# Mr Morrison's Conjuring Trick

*or*

## The People of Bethnal Green (deceased)

v
The Crown

by Rick Fountain

Published by RTFMedia
at Bromley, Kent


First print impression 2012

Cover picture is the celebrated
cartoon of Herbert Morrison, later
Baron Morrison of Lambeth
by Sir David Low
(chalk, circa 1945)
Image copyright Solo Syndication

ISBN 978-0-9572037-1-6

# PREFACE

There are many ways to begin this strange and sorry tale but perhaps the pivotal point is somewhere towards the end, at the Kings Bench division of the High Court in London and the courtroom presided over by Mr Justice Singleton. It is a bright day in July, 1944, sixteen months after the tragedy at Bethnal Green tube shelter, and the judge has been hearing a case brought by Mrs Annie Baker.

She lost her husband George and their daughter Minnie in the murderous crush on the shelter staircase a year or so previously. She has brought an action against the local council saying her loss was because of their negligence and asking for compensation.

Mysteriously, there is no press coverage as the case unfolds. The public and the reporters are kept out even though this matter, the loss of 173 lives, is of very great public interest. This piece of civil litigation is heard in secret, at the request of the attorney general, Sir Donald Somervell, acting on behalf of the home office, or perhaps its little half-sister, the ministry of home security. Both offices of state are at this time occupied by Mr Herbert Morrison, later Lord Morrison of Lambeth, a figure standing very high in the Labour party and in the wartime coalition.

We can be quite certain that the attorney general is acting for the home secretary and this should be borne in mind, as you will see. But we shall never know exactly what Sir Donald was told, nor what he said or argued in Mr Justice Singleton's courtroom because, extraordinarily, the official record never saw the light of day and, so we understand, has been destroyed.

Fortunately though, for posterity at least, although the state chose that no record should survive, we have the judgment of Mr Justice Singleton because the learned judge was sagacious enough to call in the press when the hearing had been decided. He gave an account of his verdict and it was generally summarised in the main newspapers. Those reports can perhaps still be found on smudged and scratchy microfiche records in your local library (if that too survives) and a summary also exists in the fading archives of what used to be the metropolitan borough of Bethnal Green. (It is now part of the London authority of Tower Hamlets).

'Judge says shelter steps were a trap', was one London newspaper headline. Mr Justice Singleton was slightly less succinct: "The real cause of the tragedy" he said "was the dangerou s condition of the staircase" from the street to the landing below "combined with the very poor light". Bethnal Green council had been told about the danger, he said, but ignored the warnings and so failed in its duty of care to the shelterers. It had been negligent and should compensate Mrs Baker for her loss and bereavement.

The reader may wonder several things about this but our immediate purpose should be to ask: Why is that interesting? And if it was that simple why the secrecy?

The answer, of course, is that it was not by any means that simple. Bethnal Green council had not been negligent. It had long known that there was a danger on the staircase and had repeatedly tried, well before the disaster, to make safe the access to the shelter. But its hands were tied; it was responsible for the sheltering of its little community as they endured the blitz but it could only disburse its meagre resources on safety measures when it had permission from London civil defence, the secretive, parallel government blandly entitled 'the regional commissioners' which, among much else, stood ready, in time of national calamity, to take over the functions of government. This wraith-like entity had four times dismissed the requests from Bethnal Green as a waste of money. It may be, as you will see, that its servants supposed, in 1941, that London had seen the worst of the Nazi onslaught.

Bethnal Green council could not defend itself against this charge of negligence. It found itself bound by the official secrets act, allowed only to parrot the version of what had happened which had been devised inside the ministry of home security after the accident. This official version asserted (in a muffled sort of way) that the people of Bethnal Green, Shoreditch and Stepney (widely praised as heroic during the blitz of 1940-41) had behaved, on that night of March 3, 1943, in a cowardly, hysterical fashion and had flung themselves headlong down the staircase in such numbers that they became irretrievably jammed together and quickly perished.

Mr Justice Singleton did not dilate upon the panic explanation (beyond saying that "there was nothing in the way of rushing or surging") and the idea was briskly dismissed by the Shoreditch coroner at a secret inquest. The senior police officers who gave evidence to the inquiry set up by Mr Morrison rejected the idea as did the civilian witnesses who gave evidence. However the legend was assiduously promoted to the inquiry, presided over by Mr Laurence Dunne, by a home office man, Mr Ian Macdonald Ross, who was inserted into Mr Dunne's tribunal to act as secretary. It was the version put forward by Mr Macdonald Ross, echoed in the Dunne report and endorsed by the cabinet, which has prevailed.

What is to come next in this tale may ask of you, the reader, a certain stamina. There is much detail, some dreadful, some wearying. It will be seen at almost every turn that the commonsense of the council is denied or belittled by those in power. But the matter is founded on unarguable fact; on the once-secret testimony of witnesses to the official inquiry, on long-secret cabinet papers, on treasury files, surviving fragments from the metropolitan borough of Bethnal Green, and from the ministries of home security and the home office, and the metropolitan police.

To make the matter more transparent I have set out the evidence as it might conceivably be put to a tribunal or a court hearing, in which a prosecuting counsel leads a jury through a puzzling web of documents - the raw testimony of witnesses, the Dunne inquiry report, minutes of meetings, even the inquest hearing. Here the parties are seen to explain and defend their actions and decisions. The national archives at Kew provides the bulk of the evidence but Hansard reports from parliament are also quoted.

Please remember that this is emphatically a factual work, although conjecture occurs from time to time. A reasonable jury, silently weighing the words set out by counsel, will I trust, easily separate official fact from official fiction.

Rick Fountain
London, January, 2012.

# CHAPTER 1
## Ancient History?

Ladies and gentlemen of the jury, the case you are about to hear concerns the death of one-hundred-and seventy-three people in circumstances at once tragic and terrible but also mysterious and, until now, never properly and officially ventilated. These poor people – they were mostly women and children – died in a particularly horrible way, crushed and suffocated on a dark staircase in the east end of London as they tried to escape what they thought would be another savage air assault by planes of the German air force, the Luftwaffe. The accompanying table shows the tally of the fallen at the Bethnal Green tube shelter Green at about half-past eight on the evening of March 3, 1943.

This happened at a time when Germany and Britain were at war, but if you supposed that these people were killed, like so many civilians in wartime by enemy bombing, you would be mistaken. Counsel for the people of Bethnal Green (deceased) will show you that these people went to their deaths as the result of ... well,

| Killed | |
|---|---|
| Boys under 16 years | 24 |
| Girls under 16 years | 38 |
| Women | 84 |
| Men | 27 |
| Treated in hospital | |
| Children under 16 years | 23 |
| Women | 33 |
| Men | 7 |

what shall we call it? Incompetence? Indifference? Or perhaps complacency and neglect by officials of our own government after more than three years of aerial warfare.

Further, counsel will show you that after the accident (for that is what it unmistakeably was) and an inquiry had established and reported (up to a point) upon the facts of the case, that report, even in its neutered form, was suppressed and glossed over until it had become irrelevant.

There are many charges that may be brought and these will certainly be laid before you but counsel proposes first of all to set out what can be clearly established: what happened before the accident; the conditions on the staircase; how the government strove to obscure the fact that the hazard of the staircase had been identified by local officials who wanted to insert a crush barrier at the mouth of the shelter.

Now members of the jury you will be saying to yourselves "It is too late for that; they are dead, their voices are all stilled". Sadly most of them are. So how could we reach back and revisit the scene? How can we hear the voices of those people, living and dying through the London blitz?

It is not as difficult as you might suppose. For example, the secret inquiry produced the official report which can tell us some things (although it is more interesting for what it leaves out). Much more interestingly there survives the transcript of the testimonies which helped to shape it, brought together by a London magistrate, Mr Laurence Rivers Dunne, MC. This record of his labours can be plucked from the archives (where it has lain largely unnoticed all these years) and paint for us a picture, a little stilted perhaps but, for all its sepia tinge, a compelling, evocative tapestry, recognisably the east end of London that some of our fathers and mothers might have known. We - alas! - never shall. It is a different place now, a lively, bustling place of several cultures.

So jury, let us first call up Mr Dunne;

Sir, you have looked deeply into this matter; will you tell us a little about this now-extinct metropolitan borough? As it was in the middle of March, 1943, when you stopped your questioning and started your report?

"It is almost entirely populated by the working classes" he replies.

"The vast majority of houses at the opening of hostilities were old, of no structural strength, and offering the minimum of protection against severe bombing. During the winter 1940-1941 the bombing was heavy with widespread damage and the population generally had a severe lesson in the prudence of taking cover. At the beginning of the war, three and a half years earlier, the population was about 100,000. Through evacuation this has shrunk to a little over 50,000, despite the return of some adults and a great many children."

Thank you, Mr Dunne. Let us next have the evidence given by Mr Walter Steadman, a stoker by trade, of Russia Lane, Bethnal Green.

*(The magistrate begins by asking him)*

After hearing the alert, on the evening of March 3 did you go to the shelter?" A. Yes, sir.

Q. And how far down did you go? A. To what we call the booking hall.

Q. That's to say at the bottom of the second short flight of steps. When you got there, did you stand there? A. Yes sir, because I have a weak heart

Q. Were you in fact facing the main staircase from the street? And could see people coming in? A. I walked back to the second flight, and may have been one or two steps up. I had arranged for the wife and children to come down.

Q. Looking at the people coming down the first flight you had an exceptionally good view. At this time were the people coming down as you have seen them before? A. Yes. All of a sudden I was standing watching and on the right-hand side of the people coming down I saw a woman and a child and they seemed to fall together.

Q. Were they near the bottom step? A. Perhaps two or three steps up.

Q. You noticed the woman and child fall and then what? A. There was a bald-headed man he was most conspicuous because you had to look at him. He fell on the top.

Q. Did you see any other people fall? A. It was all a-tumble. I stood there, I couldn't realise what was happening it was so quick. In a moment or two dozens of people were falling.

Q. And then I suppose, on top of these poor people other people came from the top? What did you say when these people had tumbled? A. I hollered out 'get back! let them get up' – something like that.

Q. Following this sudden fall of all of these people, did you hear any screaming? A. There was a lot of screaming and shouting. Q. Were there others with you? A. After that, there were several men standing on the platform, wardens and civilians; they ran round [but] could do nothing. We tried to pull some out but we couldn't move them.

Q. About how long was it before the police officers arrived? A. I couldn't say exactly. The first I saw of a police officer was in the dark, working on the top. I could see the black garments. I should say it was about a quarter of an hour, it might have been a little before or a little after.

Q. Subsequently you saw police officers arriving at the bottom? A. Yes.

Q. All was going quite well, people coming down in an orderly manner until this woman fell. A. Yes and in a moment there were dozens of people falling.

Thank you, Mr Steadman. Members of the jury, here was the beginning of a strange event, something unprecedented. So many people, most of them quite calm and orderly, seeking refuge in an underground place, escaping from the real hazard of a violent death by bombs from the sky, something with which they 'd been living for the previous three years. We have an outline already of this solid, immovable block of people – remember, so many of them were women and young children – and right at the base of the stairway, a couple of steps up from the landing, on the left side, we have a crucial witness, Mrs Eliza Jones, of Globe road, Bethnal Green. She had hurried to the shelter from the nearby Museum cinema when the siren sounded and found herself alive at the epicentre of the tragedy.

*(Mr Dunne, pictured facing page, asked her)*

How long do you think it took you to get to the tube shelter? A. I couldn't run because I am a bit stout, and was half frightened, and it took me about six to seven minutes.

Q. There were a lot of people about? A. Yes sir, there were.

Q. But they were going in...? A. Quite normal.

Q. And there did not seem to be any disorder? They were going in at a good speed? A. Just a level speed, as I call it sir.

Q. People were hurrying a bit in the streets to get there? A. Oh yes. I happened to get forward more perhaps than some of the others outside. I was more forward, like.

Q. You started to go quite comfortably down the stairs? A. Yes sir.

Q. When you reached the landing you had got off the first flight of stairs and on to the landing? A. The first landing, yes. As I was going round the stairs I was on the side going down, when I got to the first landing I kept round by the wall, which I always do.

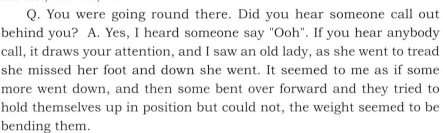

Q. Is that the left or right side? A. I went on the left, the left, sir.

Q. You were going round there. Did you hear someone call out behind you? A. Yes, I heard someone say "Ooh". If you hear anybody call, it draws your attention, and I saw an old lady, as she went to tread she missed her foot and down she went. It seemed to me as if some more went down, and then some bent over forward and they tried to hold themselves up in position but could not, the weight seemed to be bending them.

Q. Bending over people who had already fallen? A. Yes. The old lady was on about the third or fourth step, and she missed her footing, she could not see, and over she went: and as she went over she went right down on the stone, the beginning of the stone staircase, the landing. And then there were some children, a little boy I think it was, at the side of her and then some more and they all seemed to fall at the same time. Then some more bent over and they seemed to be going in like at the knee part,. Then from there they seemed to bend forward like that and all of a sudden I got hold of this boy and the old lady, I rushed to her when I got my senses and got hold of her hand and I tried to pull her off but I could not. I tried hard and I said 'never mind ma, lie there and you will be all right presently' but she could not speak and she gripped my hand. There was a man a few steps up, he was around

the wrong way as if looking up like that and saying 'don't push" or 'go back'. He was the wrong way round. There he was hollering out 'oh my back, my back, oh my head'. I thought to myself 'this is terrible' and I put my hand under him for at least a good ten minutes and my arm ached and I had to let go. This little boy, it must have been his because he kept saying 'oh my poor dad'…I said 'all right, sonny, daddy will be all right in a minute'. Then there seemed to be a rush at the top, I have never seen anything like it.

Q. Do you think the old lady who came down first was pushed over? A. I do not say she was pushed. It might have been a little bit coming in on top too much for her. I do not know for sure.

Q. You had got in ahead of her and you had not been pushed? A. I had not been pushed, no.

Q. But on the other hand, after she fell down, everybody came over her so quickly? A. Yes.

Q. It rather suggests pressure had developed there already? However, you cannot say that; all you can tell me is what you saw, and you have told me very well what you did see.


Jury this is troubling testimony you are hearing and you must steel yourself for more and worse to come. Let us now hear from a young woman, Joan Bennett, a telephonist, of Wyre House, Roman road, Bethnal Green. Like Mrs Jones, Miss Bennett had been at a cinema, the Foresters picture hall in Cambridge road with her mother. They rose to leave at once when the dismal howl of nearby air raid sirens drowned out the sounds of the film.

*(The magistrate asked)*

Miss Bennett, did the sounds of the siren clear the house? A. I couldn't say, I didn't wait to see the clearing of the house, I didn't look behind me.

Q. A lot of other people came out behind you? Were they running towards the shelter too? A. A lot of the people in the picture house come from the Mile End direction, and some from Bethnal Green, but there were not so many that came up to the tube, because I think it is really too far away for them, and there were not so many people running along by the park. I was just running myself.

Q. Why did you run on this particular night? A. Because we always go to the shelter when the warning goes. We always go to that tube shelter, and my mother was worried about my sister because she was expecting a baby this month, and she was thinking more about her, and we were running and the guns were going at the time, and I am frightened myself of the air raids, I always have been frightened, and then before we got to the tube there is an opening which goes down to the library and that whizzing was coming down, I think they say it was the new rockets, I do not know, but that whizzing was coming down.

Q. How far were you from the shelter when you heard that whizzing? A. About as far as those gates which lead down to the library in Cambridge road, about twenty to thirty yards.

Q. So you heard that noise?. A. Which we thought was a bomb coming down.

Q. Did you hear the rockets go off, that sort of whizzing roar that they make? A. I did hear the whizzing, and that is why I thought it was a bomb.

Q. When you got close to the shelter were there a lot of other people starting to run too? A. There were lots of people standing about outside the shelter.

Q. What did they do when this noise was going on? A. I couldn't say. Some were standing there and some were all running in.

Q. Did you hear anybody call out anything? A. Not at the time. I heard somebody, when I was in the crush, people calling out 'all clear' but I knew myself it was not all because I heard the guns still going from where I was. I didn't hear anybody shout out anything else.

Q. Or did you hear anybody say it was a bomb? A. No, I did not hear anything.

Q. Then you got just inside the entrance to the tube shelter. A. Yes.

Q. And up to that time you had been able to move fairly freely? A. Well we got to the shelter and I had put one foot down the first step and after that no more, I was right in the middle of the staircase, in the whole crush, and before I knew where I was, I could not turn or move or do a thing, everybody was on top of me, and I could not turn round because there were people there, I just could not turn to look behind me, and the people in front, you did not know there was a crowd there, you thought you were going into the shelter in just the usual way, and it was dark, you thought you were going to walk down as you always did, and you felt people right the way across the staircase, and when I was in that crowd I was with my mother, and my mother was at the side of me, and I had everything squeezed from inside me, and I was screaming out for help because I felt it all come from me, and by the time that had gone I turned round and looked for my mother, and I found her head going, I saw her mouth, and then I saw her head fall back.

I turned to the front and everybody was calling out 'go forward' and 'go back' you just did not know where you were, and I saw my mother was dead, I believed she was dead, but she was standing the whole time, because I was holding her.

Q. Was your mother killed? A. My mother was killed, yes, but she was standing up the whole of the time, and you were carried forward, you could not stand on your own feet.

Q. Your feet were not on the ground, but you were simply wedged upwards? A. Yes and everybody else held you and you could not even move. I had this coat on at the time and I was so hot, I could not move my arms to undo this button here and I tried to get to my mother to hold her head up. I just managed to get one hand to hold her head up, but from where I was I thought that the people were standing in the front, but I saw my brother-in-law come up from the stairs of the tube at the bottom and I saw him walk on that square platform in the front and I shouted out to him, thinking he could hear, but naturally he could not see me from where he was although I could see him, because of the reflection from the light on the stairs shining on the landing, and then...

Q. You do not know how long you were there? How long was it before you were released, Miss Bennett? A. I couldn't say. I know I came up before the all clear went.

Q. And the all clear was about nine-forty-five. A. I came out before the all clear and I wanted to stay with my mother. I was holding her up, and then before they could get her out they had to get me out first because I was wedged in with my mother, and I laid her down on the steps as they were fetching me out. I laid her down on her back. I wanted to stay with my mother to see where they were going to take her because I could not convince myself that she was dead, I just could not realise that she was dead and I wanted to stay with her, and there was a policeman there when they dragged me out ... it was the soldiers dragged me out... and he would not let me stay there and said I had to go away. He would not let me stay with her... I did not know what I was doing, I was kind of past myself, and I had one shoe on and I ran across to the shelters underneath the arches in Bethnal Green road although my house is only just a little way from the tube, I could not run back to my own place, I ran under this shelter because the guns were still going and I stayed there until the all clear went and then I ran home and told my father about it and he was just standing underneath the block where we live. He never goes to the shelter and he did not know a thing about what was going on there although we only live about fifty yards from it.

The magistrate: Miss Bennett. It has been a terrible experience. A. It is something you'll never forget.

Q. No, you will never forget it, but still the shock will disappear in time. A. I hope so, anyway.

Q. I am terribly sorry to hear about your loss and very grateful for what you have been able to tell me. Thank you so much.

Members of the jury, for many of us it is difficult to hear such painful accounts of horror and loss. Perhaps it would be better if we turned our attention, for a time, to other aspects of this episode. There are several. As is generally known - it was certainly prescribed by law, and rigorously enforced - a blackout was necessary during the hours of darkness to prevent enemy bomber pilots, as far as possible, from making out objects on the ground. There was no street lighting, buses and other vehicles travelled with lights barely brighter than a glow-worm, the windows of lighted rooms had to be blacked out, and so on. The bombers came by day as well as night but daylight raiding was more hazardous for them. Because of the black-out, there was no lighting at the mouth of the Bethnal Green shelter staircase. Let us go back to the report compiled by Mr Dunne. He tells us:

"The only lighting of this stair came from a 25-watt lamp in the bulkhead light fixed in the ceiling, which was completely obscured save for a narrow slit of far from clear glass. The cone of the light emitted was adjusted to strike the edge of the first step down and to give a dim light over the rest of the stairway. Some reflected light came from the bulkhead fitting over the landing at the bottom. The lighting was extremely dim."

Evidently, the enveloping gloom was a factor in this accident. Let us look more closely now, with the help of a senior employee of Bethnal Green council, Mr Watson Strother, who was the borough engineer. You can tell us, Mr Strother, of the council's unease about the safety of the entrance to the shelter. That was felt much earlier, it seems, eighteen months before the accident.

*(Mr Strother to Mr Dunne)* There was a recommendation submitted on August 20, 1941 to London region civil defence for dealing with the hoarding of the shelter.

Q. By hoarding,you mean the structure built up around the entrance, some sort of wooden fencing? What did you propose? A. Foundations for piers ...

Q. Mr Strother, in case the jury are a little unclear, piers in this case means strong pillars of concrete or brick, embedded in the ground to provide support for railings, or gates, or roofing and so. Please go on Mr Strother.

A. Foundations for piers, brick work, granite kerb, railings and gates of the shelter. There were a number of things that led to that. One thing was the fear of the borough council that the existing hoarding was not strong enough to prevent an inrush of people if they were determined to get in and the shelter happened to be full. Another reason was that the people had to proceed down concrete steps which, in rainy weather, were wet and likely to prove slippery. A third reason was that at the time [in 1941] the staircase was lighted simply by hurricane lamps, which were placed at the sides of the staircase.

Q. There was difficulty with hurricane lamps; they were smashed and stolen? A. That is so; and the gates at that time were not very strong and the council wanted something of a stronger character in order to prevent access if it were necessary.

Q. The gates there now, or that were there when this accident occurred, were stronger gates than had been there at the time these recommendations were put forward? A. The gates which are there now are gates which have been strengthened by the addition of bars and so on.

Q. So that it was very definitely in the minds of the borough council and their technical staff that there might be trouble at the entrance to the tube shelter? A. Yes. The council had in mind the fact that a crowd might possibly come along and endeavour to gain access, and when the gates were closed it was feared that the hoarding, as it consisted naturally of very light bars, could easily be pulled away and people could get in through the sides.

Members of the jury, Mr Strother has told us something very interesting. He has indicated that the borough council of Bethnal Green, eighteen months before this terrible tragedy, saw a possible hazard at the entrance to the tube shelter. Perhaps only in a rather cloudy, indeterminate way, the council sensed that danger lurked on the staircase;. The bellow of the sirens heralding an approaching fleet of enemy bombers, a sudden purposeful movement of people, in their hundreds, even thousands, to the shelter would create a situation extremely perilous to those more frail, such as the elderly and infirm, people with little children, and so on – those least able to negotiate this gloomy, treacherous downward passage.

And so it was, back in August 1941, that London region civil defence learned of the council's concerns. The council wrote to the regional technical adviser for the locality, Mr William Joule Kerr, and his response was critical to what was to happen later. After the accident, Mr Kerr was among those invited to attend Mr Dunne's tribunal and to face questioning. Let us hear his story now. Some of his answers are a little confusing, perhaps and you may feel that a person carrying such a burden of responsibility could have been more coherent. Here anyway is how the conversation went.

*(Mr. Dunne begins:)* Mr Kerr, you are familiar with the tube shelter here at Bethnal Green? A. Yes.

Q. I do not know if you had any part in the original design? A. Yes, I came into it fairly early. It was already a shelter when I first knew of it.

Q. Did it occur to you that it was a shelter which had features very peculiarly its own from the point of view of the large population that it would house and the fact that it had only one entrance? A. It is similar to all tube shelters that exist really in London, nearly all the station tube shelters.

Q. Nearly all the station tube shelters have only one entrance? A. Yes.

Q. And exit? A. Liverpool street is the same, it has only one entrance. It has several approaches but only one entrance into the shelter.

Q. Yes, but this has only one approach and one entrance, has it not? A. Yes.

Q. So that the whole of the shelter population would have to come in through the same gate? That is a common feature, is it? A. No, of course, there are very few shelters of this description really in London.

Q. Do you remember the correspondence which began in 1941, and certain recommendations which were put forward by Bethnal Green borough council for work to be done on the shelter? First of all, there was the suggestion for replacing the hoarding with brick, certain foundations to piers, brick work, granite kerb, re-siting some railings and repairing the gates? A. Yes.

Q. And the first scheme was in substance turned down? A. Yes.

Q. In fact you referred it to the tube people (the London transport authority) as to whether any of this work was in their opinion necessary and whether they could adapt it afterwards, and they said 'no' and you said 'Very well, we do not think it is necessary'? A. Yes.

Q. Then, Mr. Kerr, Bethnal Green council wrote a letter in which they took the matter up again, and they drew attention to that (copy of letter handed to witness) ... If you will turn to the fourth paragraph, it says, "The committee are aware, in the light of past experience, that there is a grave possibility that on a sudden renewal of heavy enemy air attack there would be an extremely heavy flow of persons seeking safety in the tube shelter, and. that the pressure of such a crowd of people would cause the wooden structure to collapse and a large number would be precipitated down the staircase. Then the next paragraph states that it is estimated in a heavy air-raid possibly 10,000 people would seek shelter in the tube, and that a serious problem would evolve in the closing of the shelter to the excess four-thousand unless some strong means of preventing their entry were provided, and then the letter goes on 'It is not unusual for most of the larger shelters in the borough to empty into the tube shelter during a heavy attack, and the committee believe there would be the possibility of a serious incident at the entrance to the tube if the responsibility remained with the personnel alone to prevent the overcrowding of the shelter. In the light of this further evidence of the need for the erection of a strong gate to the entrance, I am directed by the committee to request that further careful consideration shall be given to the matter and that approval will be granted to the erection of the gate as suggested'. Do you remember that letter being referred to you? A. Yes.

Q. What action did you take? A. I made a recommendation that the hoarding should be strengthened and the gates strengthened and that they should put a roof over the top, but the proposal was only for a nine-inch (thick) wall round the original shelter which did not come on to the path or anywhere where the crowd came. They would have to have climbed over the park railings in order to get lateral pressure on it.

Q. It seems to me that the Bethnal Green emergency committee were probably wrong in thinking that the points of danger were the hoardings round the side. A. Yes, nothing was proposed there in the way of alteration to the entrance, that is to say the gates were shown in our plan exactly as they are now.

Q. Nothing was proposed except to strengthen the gates? A. Except to strengthen the gates, and to put a lateral wall round the shelter on the inside of the park.

Q. Did you make a further examination of the shelter entrance with this letter in mind? A. Yes. I cannot give you the exact date but...

Q. You wrote a minute on October 17 'I have again inspected the approach'. Did you go round with Mr. Bridger or a member of the borough council? A. I went round with Mr. Strother.

Q. As a result of that inspection did you think that what you had sanctioned met the problem?

A. Yes, the problem they put in was from the lateral pressure from outside and I thought what I recommended was adequate for the pressure, preventing them breaking in from the sides you see.

Q. You limited really your consideration of the problem simply to lateral pressure? A. To their proposals.

Q. It did not occur to you that, in fact, the really vulnerable point was probably not the sides at all, but the front of the shelter? A. Yes I recommended that the gates should be strengthened.

Q. Having what in mind? A. It was possible they might be closed or kept half-closed.

Q. Closed? When? A. Of course, in view of later events I see now that that would have been useless because they could not have closed them against the pressure of people.

Q. But Mr. Kerr that would be elementary would it not? A. Which?

Q. That you could not close a gate against a crowd of people?

A. No, I think not, if the people are under control.

Q. Yes, but what they are envisaging is people not under control. It is directly raised here, is it not? They are envisaging such a crowd of people as would cause the wooden structure to collapse? A. Yes.

Q. Is it usual when you visit a borough council to advise them, or to base your suggestions and report on their schemes, simply to limit yourself to what they raise? A. No if anything strikes me at the time I would point it out to them.

Q. You examined, no doubt, this shelter entrance after the incident? A. Yes.

Q. Do you think it was a satisfactory entrance, having in view the number of people likely to seek shelter and the fact that there was only one entrance to take that number of people? A. In the light of events, of course, one is certainly wiser than before, but I must say that the entrance was comparable to most or many other tube shelters in London, where they deal with large crowds.

Q. Have you had any other public authority calling your attention to the fact that an entrance is extremely vulnerable to pressure from a large crowd. A. I do not remember one.

Q. This is the only one? A. Yes.

Q. Of course, if you did not apply your mind to the problem, it is no good asking you what might have influenced you at the time, but may I ask you this; why was it you only considered the proposals put forward by the borough council? Because I understand that you and your colleagues stand in a strictly advisory capacity to the borough council? A. Yes, the reason, as I said before, was that, as this was in all respects, or in a great many things similar to the entrances to tubes which are in the habit of dealing with very large crowds, I did not think it was one that called for any special treatment.

Q. Of course, the average tube is rather better lighted, is it not, the entrance to the tube, than this? That is tubes actually being used as tubes. A. Not where they enter off the street. Since the war they are just as badly lighted as this. For instance, places like Westminster, where they open off the street, you cannot light them any better than this because the light shows out in the street.

Q. At any rate, you do, when you have a problem of this nature, normally consider it in all its aspects? A. Yes

Q. Even though it may be that the authority raising the point may have missed the real point in what they have raised? A. Yes, if it had struck me, I would certainly have put it forward.

Q. That would certainly come within your view of your duties? A

Yes.

Q. To see that the steps proposed were adequate to meet the point raised? A. Yes.

Q. I suppose you have frequently problems raised and suggestions made which are insufficient, and then, of course, you put your foot down and say, "This is no good"? A. Yes, quite often.

Q. There are, in fact, very few of this type of shelter, that is to say tube underground shelters with only one entrance, only used as a shelter, and not used as a tube station? A. There are none quite as big.

Q. Have you found it necessary to put crush barriers at the entrance to many shelters? A. No, we have never done it before.

That was Mr Kerr speaking. Let us revert to the man with whom he discussed the problem, Mr Watson Strother, the borough engineer. This was his recollection of their encounter, when the magistrate asked him if the object was saving money or improving safety.

Mr Strother replied that Mr. Kerr "was of the opinion that the suggestions he'd put forward would be adequate to prevent the inrush of a crowd. That is by, where necessary, and by strengthening the gates, erecting piers and fixing strengthening bars along the hoarding".

Q. In considering this question of a sudden rush, whether by hundreds of people or several scores, did it ever strike you that the straight run-in from the pavement down those stairs offered a greater opportunity for a rush than the actual sides of the shelter, protected as they were by a light hoarding? The most vulnerable spot in the whole of your tube entrance was in fact the gateway?

A. Oh, yes, it was perfectly obvious. That was why the suggestion was made of strengthening at the gates.

Q. Did you envisage being able to close the gates in the event e of a rush? A. Half of the gate could be closed at one time, and they had also the small gate at the side which, if there were a crowd expected at the tube...

Q. You have not quite answered my question. Did you think you could possibly close any of the gates in the face of a rush? A. I cannot say what I actually thought on that point at the time, but of course obviously, looking at it in the light of experience, with a big crowd you cannot close gates of that nature in face of a rush; there is no doubt about that.

Q. But, Mr. Strother, correct me if I am wrong, what you were asked to consider was protection of the shelter in the case of a rush? A. Well, sir, there were means for closing half of the gates and allowing only a few people through at a time.

Q. Mr. Kerr, as far as you can remember, offered no criticism of that part of the scheme? - A. No, sir.

Q. That it would be quite inadequate to prevent a rush? - A. No, he offered no criticism on those lines.

Q.. The gates, at that time and since, have always opened inwards? - A. That is so, sir.

Members of the jury, it seems reasonable to suppose that although the emergency committee were clear in their own collective mind about the peril of the staircase, and what was needed, neither the civil defence man nor the engineer representing the council entirely grasped it; the leap of imagination required to picture the staircase suddenly transformed from a dark and dingy void into a bustling, swelling human channel perhaps eluded them. But jury, please note here the tenor of Mr Dunne's questioning. You will agree that he understands very well that although, as he says, the council 'may have missed the real point' he can see immediately that what they had in mind was a crush barrier. You will need to bear this in mind when analysing the report that eventually emerged from the ministry of home security. But let us proceed.

Unknown to Mr Dunne, as he questioned the eighty or so witnesses, the chief engineer of the ministry of home security, Sir Alexander Rouse, was already circulating a top-secret instruction to all regional technical advisers, requesting them to check access to any big shelters under their supervision. It was sent a week or so after the accident and copied to Mr Kerr.

From his office at the ministry, Sir Alexander told all technical advisers to start re-evaluating the entrances to large shelters in their areas. He began with a request for extreme secrecy - "for the moment nothing should be said to the local authorities.

"In order that you may understand how the trouble occurred, I attach a rough sketch of the entrance to the Bethnal Green shelter." (This sketch does not survive.)

"The entrance from the street leads to an underground booking hall such as is common on the tube railways. From the booking-hall there are escalators down to the tube level. As you will notice the gates of the shelter are directly on the pavement and the entrance stairs are covered by a corrugated iron roof supported on brick piers between which there are rather rough wooden panels. The staircase was dimly lit and for blackout reasons more light could not be given.

"Normally, the shelter is used by persons with tickets who spend the night in the shelter. On the night of the accident, there was an alert and many people in the neighbourhood and off the streets made for the shelter.

"A woman fell near the bottom of the steps, and about this time the (anti-aircraft) barrage in the neighbourhood started, making people anxious to get under cover, with the result that in a matter of seconds the people were piled up on the stairs, and the crowd (by no means a large one) could not be checked at the entrance, the doors of which opened inwards.

"The shelter and the entrance were not designed for shelter purposes but were adaptations of the London passenger transport board's ordinary arrangements, and the shelter had been in use since the beginning of the war. No incident had occurred, although the bunk capacity of the shelter is 5,000, and as many as 10,000 had taken cover at times in the shelter.

"You will remember that the entrances to shelters in the early days were designed in such a way that persons caught in the streets or living nearby could enter the shelter within seven minutes. In the winter of 1940-41 this idea of people taking cover on the alert became more or less obsolete, and the demand from a certain proportion of the population was for sleeping accommodation in a shelter which people occupied over a period about blackout time, and the width of entrances became of less moment.

"A new phase has now occurred owing to the absence of continuous raiding and to the appearance of the 'tip-and-run' raider. Although a few still go to spend the night in large shelters, the majority have reverted to a condition more approximate to the original conception, and want to get off the street or away from their houses for the period of the alert only. There is, therefore, the necessity to re-examine the entrances to large shelters with this in view.

"In the particular instance of Bethnal Green the bottleneck to the shelter occurs at the top of the lone flight of escalators which are stationary and only two of which have treads, the third being closed. It is useless, therefore, to allow a crowd to come in off the street to the booking-hall at a rate which only transfers the pressure to the head of the escalators, and, in any scheme for the improvement of entrances, it is desirable to have adequate means of control at the entrance so that the rate of entry shall not exceed that which any bottleneck within the shelter can cope with.

"The following, therefore, are the points at which you should look at in examining the entrances to shelters:-

• Are the blackout arrangements such that it is possible to give good lighting on any points of danger such as staircases or steep slopes?

• Are there means of controlling entry of a crowd so that there is not undue pressure at the bottleneck or at the head of staircases and steep slopes? For example, a useful method of closing the entrance is a double (concertina-type metal) gate closing on a stout central pillar (e.g., six-by-six timber) so that the warden stationed at the pillar can pull the gates across in case of any trouble.

• Are staircases or steep ramps provided with handrails? In the case of wide entrances (say over seven or eight feet) are central handrails provided to divide the traffic into lines and provide the shelterers with something to hang on to when going downwards?

• Are there sufficient means of communication to enable wardens or police to control a crowd in the case of trouble on the stairs or at bottlenecks within the shelter?

"For the moment you should confine yourself to reviewing the conditions at very large shelters where a situation such as I have described might occur. It is obvious that such trouble is not likely to arise in dormitory shelters situated at considerable distance from densely populated areas.

"Official orders on this matter will issue when the enquiry is complete, but in the meantime I should like to have your views as to whether there are any shelters in your region which you consider require attention, together with a brief description and sketches illustrating your opinion".

Sir Alexander's letter is an admirable summary of what had happened and sensible measures to be taken, although you will have noted that, presumably to blur the actual facts (which were then top secret) he identified the bottleneck as being lower down, in the booking hall. We have seen, and we can be sure that Sir Alexander saw, that the primary danger was on the first dark and overloaded stairway. The entrance was wider than the stairway and it acted as a funnel.

Let us now return to Mr Dunne's inquiry and hear from Mr Percy Bridger, a Bethnal Green councillor at this time, and a former mayor. When he took the stand, Mr Dunne began by asking if it had ever struck him that trouble might arise because of a rush for cover from the street?

Mr Bridger: We always managed to get large numbers of people in without any difficulty. There has always been the (same) entrance, booking hall and escalators; when the shelter has been filling it has always been full of people all the way down, as it was that evening, but there has never been any difficulty, never any real stoppage. We always managed to get them in quite well.

Q. Has it ever crossed your mind that you might have difficulty, a rush? A. Going back, of course, it has been considered that something might be done to lessen the danger.

Q. When was that discussed or brought up? A. It was considered by the emergency committee ... it must be quite eighteen months ago. All through the (1940-41) blitz this actual staircase was in the open air, without any lighting except two hurricane lamps. That was the only light we were allowed, and it was pretty well blacked out.

Q. It was not until you turned [at the bottom of the first flight] that you had any permanent cover at all?

A. [When it rained] we had a man sweeping at the bottom of the stairs because of puddles and as a result of that and the bad light we considered something ought to be done to improve the entrance and we made representations to have a covering put over and also some gates to be fitted which would prevent any danger of panic. The result was that we had the present covering put over, and wooden doors fitted.

Q. What gates had you in mind to relieve the pressure? A. At that time we were afraid that we might be overwhelmed with more people than the shelter could take, and, of course, that still may apply. After all, you cannot get a quart into a pint bottle, and although we have got bunking for five-thousand people, the estimated standing room would probably give us another five-thousand. There are fifty-thousand people in Bethnal Green and with the altered conditions, the barrage and everything else, and people becoming more alarmed, you are likely to get many more people wanting to come in.

Q. So it did occur to you and the emergency committee that you might have dangerous pressure on the entrance? A. Yes, that was freely discussed and recommendations were made.

Q. And, in fact, nothing was done? A. What was done was that present cover ...

Q. The cover was put there, but as regards a barrier or anything to relieve the pressure, nothing was done? A. Wooden doors were put up after the surrounds had been made, mostly in timber, and there were some piers built to give strength to the wooden partitions, and then, of course, we did get a little lighting but until that we had no lighting at all, but even with the small amount of lighting we were able to put in we had complaints that light was streaming over the pavement.

Q. On another matter, councillor Bridger, I don't think anything turns here on nationalities, but you have great experience of this shelter ,,, have you found that any particular kind of people are more difficult to deal with or more likely to get excited or to lose their heads?

A. So far as nationalities are concerned we have been quite free of any trouble in that connection, for instance, we have only I suppose perhaps one in a hundred jewish people. It is quite as small as that.

Q. As a regular population of your shelters? A. Yes. Of course, you get the rougher elements to deal with, and we have had to deal with them from time to time, that is in regard to their conduct in the shelter, but by taking a firm hand and threatening exclusion, and in one or two cases we have excluded people, we have been able to prevent any rough play. You always get those kinds of people to deal with in a large crowd. Generally speaking the people have always been very friendly, they have always appreciated the fact that they had such a good shelter and we have never had any difficulty, people have been under proper control.

At various points in the transcripts, Mr Dunne seizes an opportunity to test his own notions of how such a horrible accident might be avoided; typically, for a military man and a lawyer, and pre-occupied with matters of order and control, he conceived that the method of slowing the hurrying crowds could be a mechanical one – a system of traffic lights, red for stop where you are and green for keep moving. But when he put it to the several senior police officers who came before him, suggesting that it would be obediently observed he was disillusioned. Sub-Div. Insp Jannaway bluntly dismissed it: "A red light would not be effective". Chief Insp. Harris was more diplomatic but equally categoric: "Red lights would not work" he declared. "People would not pay attention to it."

Mr Dunne: "You think the only reliable measure is a crush barrier to relieve pressure from the street?" "Yes."

# CHAPTER 2
## The Ministerial Analysis

In the aftermath of what happened at Bethnal Green, opinion and advice flowed freely to the ministry of home security from both official and unofficial sources. For example, one person much better placed than most to make recommendations was the metropolitan police commissioner, air-vice marshal Sir Philip Game. He knew the East End well, he knew about the control of crowds, and he knew, we can be sure about the limits and possibilities of military air power. He'd served as a staff officer under Trenchard in the Royal Flying Corps, and was a distinguished administrator long before he took over at the Yard.

A month after the tragedy, Sir Philip wrote briefly to Herbert Morrison, home secretary and minister for home security, offering his view that the outstanding lesson from what had happened "is the desirability of taking every possible step to prevent the application of pressure by persons outside the entrances and awaiting admittance upon those who have reached and are occupying the internal approaches or stairways." This could be achieved Sir Philip said, "by the marshalling of would-be shelterers by the police, or the provision of suitably placed crush barriers or gates."

Members of the jury, as we have seen, this excellent advice was very much in line with what the councillors and the town clerk of Bethnal Green had proposed. But it did not fit in with the ministerial analysis; it clashed uncomfortably with Mr Morrison's presentation to the full cabinet, on April 5, 1943, of his version of Mr Dunne's findings, and his projection of an alternative explanation, a 'psychological' theory which, once adopted, would allow the matter to take on the full official majesty of a state secret.

But jury here, perhaps, we are going forward too fast. You will know that loss of civilian life by aerial attack (and later by flying bombs and v-2 rockets) in wartime London, and other cities, was a recurring reality. Here though on this dark staircase was something mysteriously different and the public questioning at once arose – how could such a thing happen? And might this have been avoidable? Let us look at the chronology.

For most people, word of the tragedy came thirty-six hours after it happened, on the morning of Friday, March 5. Officialdom moved more quickly. A mere nine or so hours after the last bodies had been lifted away from the staircase, a secret conference was under way at the town hall, under the chairmanship of the London region civil defence boss, Sir Ernest Gowers. Six of his people were there, including Mr Kerr, from whom we have heard, and the man actually in charge of London civil defence works, Charles Key. An official record of what was said was taken by Mr Ian Macdonald Ross, an aide to Mr Morrison.

Others included the mayor of Bethnal Green, Mrs Margaret Bridger, the town clerk Stanley Ferdinando, Mr Strother, borough engineer and half a dozen councillors. The ministry of home security was represented by Sir Alexander Rouse and a ministerial aide, Mr Arthur Edmunds; the London passenger transport board, and the ministries of information and pensions were also present. Sir Ernest, a distinguished Whitehall veteran, enjoined all present to secrecy - it was "most important at this stage" he said, that no information be given to the press regarding the disaster. After the formalities, Sir Ernest proposed an adjournment to let safety specialists work out practical measures.

They met again in the afternoon and this time Sir Alexander Rouse set out plans to install a new passage leading into the shelter and on to the staircase. Curiously enough what follows does not appear in the home office files but turned up among papers in the Bethnal Green archives which, at the time of writing, are to be found at the Bancroft Road library in Stepney Green. This is part of what the minutes of that March 4 meeting recorded:

"The chief engineer of the ministry of home security submitted a plan ... showing a structure which had been agreed upon together with the borough engineer, the regional technical advisor, the regional works advisor, and officers of the London passenger transport board which he suggested would prevent any similar accident in the future.'

"The plan showed the suggested covered entrance to the staircase to be placed in the Bethnal Green gardens (the little park adjoining the present tube station) which was of such length as to ensure that persons entering the shelter came in at some distance from the head of the staircase; this covered entrance would act as a blast-proof and splinter-proof subsidiary shelter to protect persons entering. An additional advantage, it was pointed out, would be that the entrance would be removed from the corner (at the top of the staircase). The chief engineer further stated that the approximate cost would be £500.."

Counsel cannot show members of the jury any images of what emerged and it was of course dismantled long ago when the war ended. But it seems to have been a covered, possibly u-shaped corridor which turned into the staircase itself. This and the staircase could now be adequately lit and, as before, led down to the booking hall on the intermediate floor. The number of escalators from that floor down to the platforms where shelterers waited, was increased from two to three.

Jury some among you may be asking yourselves: Why so much detail of this? Surely this is a trivial matter, not worth dwelling upon at such length. Counsel would suggest to you that this is not at all trivial; this was the response that should have been made if the hazard had been perceived and acted upon by those with the specific responsibility; if it had been put into place by an energetic and astute civil defence official eighteen months earlier, so many lives, and so much heartache would have been spared. And of course, whatever was said later, to disparage and explain away the warnings from the borough council, the indisputable fact remains that the expert official remedy so belatedly arrived upon was manifestly a superior version of what the council had asked for. Take note also of the name of Mr Ian MacDonald Ross, mentioned above. His was the record of what we learn from this meeting and he also figures in what came next, the secret inquiry conducted by Mr Dunne.

There is no mention in the official files of the status of Mr Macdonald Ross, but perhaps we should see him, in this case at least, as the minister's crisis manager – and also as the person assigned to manage Mr Dunne's findings.

But first, Mr Dunne himself. At a public meeting at Bethnal Green after the tragedy, local people demanded an immediate public inquiry presided over by a judge. In our own time it would have been absolutely unacceptable for anyone other than such a person, someone of the highest judicial standing, to lead an inquiry. It would certainly have taken longer than it took Mr Dunne, and a home office minder might well have found such a person harder to steer. The man that Mr Morrison, assigned to the task was the resident magistrate at the Bow street court, an accomplished legal practitioner, of course, but not a person with the political and judicial authority of a judge. Mr Dunne had many qualities but he could not nowadays be seen to be an acceptable choice.

At his death in 1960, an obituarist was to describe Mr Dunne thus: "He was a sound lawyer who thought clearly and pleaded succinctly. In court his manner was relaxed, civil, but never obsequious. His prose was elegant, terse, and authoritative. A man of conventional good looks, with a soldierly bearing, who was convivial in male company and commanded a store of legal anecdotes, he was popular both on the western circuit and at the Garrick club. Fly-fishing was his absorbing interest; he seemed to prefer the company of trout to jurors, witnesses, or even judges".

Here is another, less formal and perhaps more revealing, glimpse of the style of Mr Dunne, from the transcript of what he asked and was told as he questioned a succession of some eighty persons at the Bethnal Green secret inquiry. A word of caution; jurors should remember that this was 1943 and here is Mr Dunne in a relaxed, near-jovial frame of mind, speaking with superintendent Hill of H Division, metropolitan police. The exchange nicely reflects the now-forgotten habits of the British empire, as it then was, rather than current notions of racial protocol.

Mr Dunne: Now generally, the population has been well-behaved during the blitz?

Supt. Hill: Extremely well.

Q. They have been sensible, self-controlled and really have made the task of the police comparatively easy? A. Yes. I feel bound to say, before the blitz started badly in1940, I wondered, because I have a big foreign element in this division and I had a certain amount of apprehension but it was all needless because they took it extremely well.

Q. More as a matter of interest, because I do not think it has been suggested in any reports, have you noticed any difference in the behaviour of different nationalities, or races, generally speaking? A. I cannot say that I have. It must be said that at the outbreak of the blitz a good deal of the jewish population left London, particularly they slept out of London and came back to business during the day but those who remained behind were as well-behaved as our ordinary population.

Q. No more likely to panic? A. No. Like most people they are in a hurry to get to the shelters.

Q. They are rather more excitable I think perhaps than the average? A. Rather more excitable, rather talkative.

Q. Rather more than the fellow we call the cockney, the real good old cockney? A. That is what we have here at Bethnal Green that is why we have little panic here. I must say even the jew, contrary to what we believed, he is a bit excitable and his womenfolk get a bit excited, but they stood up to it extremely well. They surprised me and everybody else who knows this part of London.

Q. When you speak of the foreign element, is it the jew you are speaking of? A. Yes,

Q. Actually apart from them, there are only a few foreigners? A. I have a big chinese population at Limehouse and I must say they are the worst.

Q. Have you got any considerable section of the population who do not speak English?

A. Not a large number.

Q. They are mostly second and third generation jews? A. Yes, some of the older jews do not speak english but they are able to make themselves understood.

Q. I notice when they come to a police court they very often forget all their english, but I think that is more in the nature of protection. A. I am afraid they forget when they want to.

Q. At any rate, .you think there is no question that the people who do not speak english are a minority, an inconsiderable section of the population? A. Quite.

These exchanges, so very unlikely to be heard in a public place nowadays, help to create a picture in our minds of both these men; but notice also that the superintendent is emphatic in asserting that the people do not panic. This assertion, made also in the press and by other witnesses, will be inconvenient to the government since the wish at the ministry of home security, as we shall see, was to establish a narrative that those entering the shelter on that night of March 3 were in the grip of uncontrollable fear; they had "lost their self-control" and because of that supposed hysteria had brought their deaths upon themselves. This myth of the loss of self-control, as we shall see, was soon to be adopted by the minister as a psychological flaw in the makeup of the people of the east end that might threaten the conduct of the war.

Counsel has pored laboriously over the many pages of transcript accumulated from the testimony of witnesses; very few, possibly only one or two among those who gave evidence to Mr Dunne supported the idea that there had been anything approaching a stampede. Authority however, in the shape of the ministry, insisted that there had been and on this premise was built a reason to declare a 'psychological' cause for what had happened. This was offered to the cabinet by Mr Morrison to advance the notion that if the enemy knew what had happened – that is to say, there really had been a panic – this would encourage him into exploiting this by deliberately bombing in the proximity of entrances to other London air raid shelters that were configured in the same way, so driving the terror-stricken, fleeing populace to destruction.

To those of you, members of the jury, who have read about, or seen, or experienced something like the terrible mayhem of the blitz, this notion will seem far-fetched, bordering upon the preposterous. The direction-finding devices available to bomber pilots at that time could not have provided the accuracy needed for such a project, nor would the fuel reserves which governed the flying-times of bomber aircraft have encouraged it. No expert evidence appears on any of the files from any practitioner in psychiatric medicine or in psychology; nor is there any opinion from any military aviator. Perhaps air-vice marshal Sir Philip Game could have been asked about this notion? There is no sign that he was.

There is another flaw possibly even more fatal to the 'psychology' explanation; it proposed that aerial terrorism could goad Londoners into a madness that sent them scrambling headlong into the shelters elsewhere in such numbers that many would be crushed and suffocated as they had been at Bethnal Green. But as Mr Kerr admitted, the Bethnal Green shelter was unique; it was the only really big deep shelter which had only the one entrance. The scenes on the staircase could not be re-created elsewhere.

But jury, the reasoning put forward by the minister of home security was not for public examination or discussion. While the war and the external threat endured, it was to be whispered only to the innermost few, those in the cabinet, something to exist only in a secret file, a reason that only a few might be told, that would allow or justify spreading a national security blanket over the episode. The public could not be allowed to know, not in 1943 at least, when the outcome of the war was still uncertain, that the real explanation for the Bethnal Green disaster was that the civil defence system had suffered a critical failure.

At first sight, jury, you might think that shrewd, forceful people such as ministers and their advisers could not seriously countenance such a bogus 'state secret'; that it would be too absurd, risible; but there is no question that it was solemnly adopted by the ministry, nodded through by the cabinet and then lovingly and faithfully nurtured and reiterated through thick and thin, even until our own times.

We shall return to that, jury, but at this point let us look at how the magistrate, Mr Dunne, set about compiling the draft of his report which was then delivered into the ministerial hand. In a somewhat reconstructed form it reached the war cabinet on April 3.

The investigator opened the hearings on Thursday, March 11, 1943 and sat for six of the following seven days, concluding on the following Wednesday, the 17th. He saw some eighty witnesses, starting with senior police officers and council officials. The key testimony from Mr Kerr, Mr Strother and Sir Alexander Rouse was given on the penultimate day, Tuesday, March 16. Shorthand writers, probably supplied from the treasury, took notes but none was continuously present. Others – the two local MPs, council officers and the town clerk of Bethnal Green, Mr Stanley Ferdinando - were allowed in but the record does not show how continuous their presence was. It was Mr Ferdinando who signed the four letters from the council and it would be reasonable to assume that he might have been able to tell the inquiry just what it was that the council feared. But he was not invited to speak.

Only one other person sat throughout: he was Mr Ian Macdonald Ross of the home security ministry, the designated secretary of the inquiry. There was of course no press coverage. The draft of Mr Dunne's report went to the ministry, we know not when and then, some days later, a summary of some of its conclusions was sent to the cabinet. The draft that survives on the file includes, beyond the recitation of the bald physical details of the calamity, an account of the correspondence between the local council and the civil defence people about the danger of congestion at the entrance and what might have been done to rectify it. Mr Dunne discusses this without attaching much significance to it. But jury let me draw to your attention the closing paragraphs of the report which, counsel contends are completely against the logic and the flow of what has gone before.

In the 62nd paragraph the document says:

62. May I conclude with two short propositions?

(a) This disaster was caused by a number of people losing their self control at a particularly unfortunate place and time.

(b) No forethought in the matter of structural design or practicable police supervision can be any real safeguard against the effects of a loss of self control by a crowd. The surest protection must always be that self control and practical common sense, the display of which has hitherto prevented the people of this country being the victims of countless similar disasters.

That reference to self-control occurs in both 'propositions'; and, as we have seen, the civil defence chiefs ordered instant changes to the way into the shelter, to slow down and channel the hurrying crowds. Please compare, members of the jury, the remark about 'no forethought in the matter of structural design' with what officialdom actually did when confronted with the facts arising from the accident. It sounds either dishonest or foolish and Mr Dunne was not either of those. So how was this mysterious 'proposition' brought about? How was this capable lawyer and decorated soldier steered away from his task to find out the truth. Did he in fact support this untruth? Or perhaps merely acquiesce in something pressed upon him as being in the overriding national interest? Let us look more piercingly at the secret process that Mr Morrison, or his people, set in train.

Perhaps the most significant figure in the tribunal was Mr Morrison's man, Ian MacDonald Ross. He had the title secretary but the surviving papers suggest that his brief was not to assemble, organise and collate but to shape the findings of the inquiry, to steer the Dunne report into a narrative that would absolve London civil defence; to establish, so far as might be accomplished, that the death of 173 people, jammed and suffocated on a darkened staircase, was the inevitable consequence of their own headlong flight. Their alleged 'loss of self-control' could then be used to explain what had happened and to justify the suppression of the fact that the danger had been foreseen and then neglected, and to pretend instead that a 'psychological' explanation had been uncovered which a cunning and ruthless enemy would exploit.

To this end, members of the jury, Mr MacDonald Ross prepared a briefing document, which is now presented to you. It looks ordinary enough and, on reading, it is easy to pass it over as insignificant. But it is not at all insignificant; it is a prime part of the evidence because it shows how the Ministry of Home Security reshaped the official narrative, to move it away from the cold logic that too many people were trying to occupy the same space at the same time.

This flimsy document lies inside one of the many home security files on the tragedy, five pages of copy paper. Here and there the typist has evidently been instructed to leave blank spaces to be filled in later by another hand. That hand, we can be sure, was that of Mr Macdonald Ross and and it inserts words into the document presumably deemed too delicate, or perhaps too tendentious, for a lowly clerk or typist to see. What were these words, members of the jury? Let us embark on a little enterprise of detection.

In all the surviving papers on the Bethnal Green tragedy there are very few signs of conspiratorial activity. Here however, counsel suggests, is one of the few tangible pieces of evidence to show how the trick was done, the creation of a body of material in the mind of Mr Dunne, the investigator, an explanation of how 'psychological' causes could be attributed to the shelter tragedy.

The paper comes out of nowhere; there is no sign that it was requested or commissioned and it is not acknowledged by Mr Dunne. Perhaps it is the fruit of a conversation between Mr Dunne and Mr Macdonald Ross.

At the top of the first of these five typed pages, these handwritten words appear:

```
Mr Dunne Perhaps the general
'lay-out' could be something on these lines.
Ian Macdonald Ross 15/3
```

S E C R E T

(First draft)

Suggested items for report

I introductory

(1) remit
(2) brief description of shelter and entrance (to be amplified later) and of accepted facts and results of accident. Quote casualty figures at date of report.
(3) fuller description of shelter. Detailed description of entrance. Plan, steps, lighting, handrails, etc., at date of accident.
(4) general staffing arrangements.
(5) use of shelter prior to 3rd March. Mostly "dormitory".
II narrative
(6) (a) position prior to alert on 3rd March
    (b) position between alert and gunfire.
    (c) position immediately following gunfire - rush, block, compression, etc.
    (d) period between beginning of disaster and partial clearance at head of stairs.
    (e) brief description of rescue operations.
    (f) confirmation of narrative from medical evidence

III causes
(7) (a) excessive reliance on deep shelter generally; this borough had sixty per cent of its public shelter in the tube and certainly a larger percentage than any of the neighbouring boroughs. Apart from the regular users, there was a large number of persons who looked on it as a second line of reserve against particularly heavy raiding. As a whole, the population tended to be "tube minded".
    (b) The shelter, for its size, was, if not unique, at least very exceptional, in relying on one entry with one

staircase. This defect was inherent in the structure of the shelter and probably does not admit of improvement. (cf, possible jam on escalators and also lower down).

(c) There were three strong psychological factors which contributed to the event. The first was the apprehension of drastic reprisals for the bombing of Berlin: this apprehension seems to have been accentuated by press accounts of the destructive effect of 8,000lb bombs.

(d) Secondly, a fear of the effects of the new barrage and a desire to "get under cover" — however light — at all costs. (Alongside this is the first handwritten insertion) Shelter entrance exposed

(e) Thirdly, the presence in the borough of large numbers of children who had returned since the 1940/41 blitz: the presence of their children had induced a number of the witnesses to seek cover which they would not otherwise have sought. The actual presence of children in the crush aggravated the position and no doubt helped to precipitate ... (handwritten word) .. "panic.."(inserted here.)

(f) A further aggravation came from the new type of raid where the interval between sirens and bombs has been reduced. There was an urge to get to cover quickly before the raid developed.

(g) There was a fairly widespread impression in the crush that the shelterers were being deliberately held back and that the "doors" or "gates" had been shut; this impression may have been partly instinctive at the time but it may, and I think probably was, reinforced by the knowledge that on previous occasions the flood gates had been closed as people were entering. I think there is no doubt about that.

(h) The lighting on the stairs was certainly not ideal and the semi-darkness conduced to increase confusion and (inserted) ..produce panic...

(i) The absence of a crush barrier gave a "straight run in"

(j)  handrails ?

Most  of  these  factors  applied  in  the  case  of  other
shelters,  but  almost  certainly  not  all  of  them  to  any  other
shelter.  All  the  necessary  precedents  for  a  ....  (inserted)
..panic...  were  present  at  Bethnal  Green  and  on  a
retrospective  analysis  of  the  situation  it  appears  probable
that  the  accident  was  more  likely  to  happen  at  this
particular  shelter  at  this  particular  time  than  at  any
other  shelter  at  any  other  time.  There  is  room  for  surprise
that  the  accident  did  not  happen  before  March  3  and  there
is  also  room  for  fearing  that  it  may  recur  elsewhere
(unless  suitable  precautions  are  taken)  in  the  event  of
"concentration"  raids.

IV  false  explanations  of  the  incident

(h) The lighting on the stairs was certainly not
ideal and the semi-darkness conduced to increase
confusion and ....................✓

(i) The absence of a crush barrier gave a
"straight run in" ✓

(j) Handrails ? ✓

Most of these factors applied in the case of
other shelters, but almost certainly not all of
them to any other shelter. All the necessary
precedents for a .......................
..............................were present at Bethnal
Green and on a retrospective analysis of the

(9)   jewish panic
(10)  panic engineered by criminal elements or fascists
(11)  (handwritten)...  Accidental collapse of crowd without

p39

panic owingto fall of woman near foot of stairs ....

V complaints made to inquiry regarding contributory factors

(12) no lighting. This is not the case. Explain dimming of bulkhead light; light probably was inadequate but shelterers' complaints were always in the contrary sense.

(13) short sill. There may have been something in this but its importance can be overstressed. The incident might have occurred with a considerably longer run in though perhaps not on quite such a large scale.

(14) additional entrances no? This would have helped at the entrances but would have made difficulties further down

(15) no handrails - there were handrails on one side. Several witnesses noticed the rail on the left hand side which suggests that it was shown up by light from the landing and not by the bulkhead light. (handwritten, alongside text) .. stairs dangerous.

(16) lack of police at entrance - Put in its strongest form this complaint suggests that control knew the imminence of reprisal raids and should have had police posted. I think there is substance in this. But how many police would they have posted and could they have controlled the crowd?

(17) lack of wardens at head of stairs - But they could probably have done little in the event and they were concentrated at the most likely bottleneck.

(18) need of general strengthening of police and wardens services. This is probably impracticable in present manpower situation.

(19) failure of wardens to do anything effective at foot of stairs. This is unfair. Probably nobody could have prevented the collapse and certainly nobody could have extricated the people immediately, once the pile-up started.

VI functioning of services

(20) (a)  wardens
     (b)  police
     (c)  ambulances
     (d)  heavy and light rescue
     (e)  communications

VII proposals made to region by borough council in 1941

(21) (a)  gist of correspondence

(b)  did emergency committee foresee the real problem? if so, they suggested wrong remedy and why did they let the matter drop?

(c)  did region foresee the problem? If not, was this due to exclusive consideration of the council's proposals? or because the rush on the siren was not foreseen? Was it reasonable to expect region to predict the difficulty in the autumn-winter of 1941?

VIII steps taken or proposed to prevent recurrence

(22) (a)  description of covered way in removing congestion into the open where it can be controlled.

(b)  lighting of covered, way and entrance.

(c)  crush barrier

(d)  handrails

(23) consideration should be extended to case of all large public shelters with stairways - this is necessary in view of changed raiding conditions (now reproducing those forecast in Hailey report)and because of the new barrage.

IX complaints about general administration of shelter

(24) (a)  complaints about internal administration of shelter were for the most part outside the ambit of the inquiry but there is a fair body of evidence to suggest that a "jam" occurred, or at least was developing in January raid - this is related to question of flood gates which requires further examination.

(b)  wearing of uniform by wardens - this should be more strictly enforced

(c)  entry of duty times - this should surely be done under supervision

(d)  recording of messages - the usual operational procedure should be followed

(e)  these and one or two other points suggest that while the administration of the shelter was not noticeably unsatisfactory it was not on the other hand, conspicuously efficient.

(f) while therefore it is probable that many of the criticisms were actuated by political motives or personal animus and while many of them were demonstrably unfounded, it would be a prudent measure on the part of the regional commissioners and/or the ministry of health to satisfy themselves that every possible improvement of organisation is introduced into this large and important shelter at the earliest possible date. In particular they should seriously consider whether it is desirable in the public interest that members of a local authority should hold executive office under the council, for example as shelter wardens.

25. Summary and conclusion
keynote to whole incident — antecedent conditions for (handwritten word) ... panic... precipitated by (handwritten)... discharge of rocket guns .. at a particularly unfortunate place and time.

At this point, this document ends. Members of the jury we can agree, I think, that some parts of this paper are a puzzle and there appears to be impropriety. It is dated March 15, five days after Mr Dunne had begun questioning his witnesses. Now it seems, the assistant assigned to him by the ministry whose responsibility for the shelter is under scrutiny, has taken to defining what happened and guiding Mr Dunne away from what may seem to us, at this distance, the obvious explanation: That in a shelter which up to ten-thousand people might suddenly need as a refuge, far too many people were allowed to press on, unchecked, into a single, dimly-lit staircase. Bethnal Green borough council had seen this and had shown this; but the government experts, the professionals, theoretically well aware of the need for anxious crowds to be carefully channelled, had not.

Maybe it indicates that someone inside the ministry had begun to apprehend that Mr Dunne, a highly-educated man, distinguished soldier and experienced lawyer, could not be trusted to arrive without guidance at conclusions favourable to its case; if the paper on the file was designed merely to help him get at the truth of what had happened, it was more than a little late; the process was already well under way and was producing, as the transcripts show, evidence that supported the accuracy of what had been predicted and what had happened, in harrowing detail.

What did not emerge from the testimony, in any convincing way, was evidence of real panic that Mr Macdonald Ross was so assiduously promoting, that the shelterers were other than merely anxious and purposeful as they hastened to the refuge. The minister's man was sitting in the tribunal and hearing the testimony; and yet in his paper he could list, in section IV 'false explanations of the incident' in his own handwriting, what must surely be the central fact in the drama - Accidental collapse of crowd without panic owing to fall of woman near foot of stairs. Every account of what happened – press reports at the time, witnesses, even the official statement afterwards, concentrate on this. How could that be a false explanation? You will also have noted, members of the jury that Mr Macdonald Ross asks the question: 'did emergency committee foresee the real problem? if so, they suggested wrong remedy and why did they let the matter drop?' But he would have seen the papers and certainly should have known that the local council raised the matter four times in the space of six months. How many warnings can one give?

# CHAPTER 3
# The Psychology Notion

Some of the official papers on this affair have long been in the public domain so any diligent researcher could have arrived at conclusions similar to those now being set out before you. But until relatively recently, a key element was missing; how did the story play at the highest level of government? For instance, how did the cabinet react? Was the responsible minister, Mr Morrison, under pressure? Or was he able to manage the thing the way he wanted? Perhaps he sought another outcome but found himself blocked? His power, after all, though great was not unlimited. Doubts in cabinet could have stopped him in his tracks. Let us see then, members of the jury, how the matter played out on those two occasions when the Bethnal Green tragedy appeared on the cabinet agenda.

We have a briefing note from the files of what Mr Morrison proposed to say to his cabinetcolleagues at the discussion five days after the event. We do not know if he actually spoke to this, as they say, but here are the words:

The case for an independent inquiry is:-

It cannot be taken for granted, and the public does not take it for granted, that official negligence or faulty structural or administrative arrangements may not be among the contributory causes of this incident. Since such a possibility exists, the local authority, the region and the ministry may all be implicated and it is therefore desirable that enquiry into the circumstances should be independent. Argument in favour of public hearing

(1) In the absence of reasons to the contrary, any enquiry into a matter of public interest should be in public.

(2) Since public opinion is roused and stirred by the extraordinary nature and results of this incident, a public enquiry would have a reassuring effect; while a private enquiry might suggest that the Government felt there was something to hide.

(3) There is a public demand in Bethnal Green and in sections of the ress for a public inquiry.

Argument in favour of a private hearing

(1) Matters of security may be raised. (These parts of the inquiry could however be held privately in any case.) Nevertheless, things bearing on British psychology under strain is of value to the enemy.

(2) The effect on public morale of a continued rehearsal in the daily press of horrible details and suggestions of panic and fear would be bad. The curious (handwritten word unclear) of the press might be insufficient to lessen this.

(3) A public enquiry might be used by irresponsible or disaffected local interests or personages as an opportunity for propaganda.

(4) We are at war.

The paper is initialled 'SoS' presumably secretary of state, and dated March 8. Already Mr Morrison is here raising the spectre of a large and public row over blame for the deaths and we can be sure that collectively, the cabinet preferred that the matter should be dealt with as quickly, cleanly and quietly as possible.

This war cabinet, of course, was an administration more incisive and focused than any peacetime counterpart and it was peopled by numerous heavyweights; Clement Attlee, the Labour party leader and MP for a constituency adjoining Bethnal Green, was Churchill's deputy; Anthony Eden was foreign secretary; Ernie Bevin, the former union boss was minister for labour; the formidable marxist intellectual, Sir Stafford Cripps, was minister for aircraft production; Sir John Anderson and Sir Kingsley Wood were respectively lord president of the council and chancellor of the exchequer. For all practical purposes, there was no parliamentary opposition.

We have seen how Mr Morrison planned his discourse ahead of the cabinet discussion; what is more recent was the release of the verbatim account of cabinet exchanges at this time which emerged from what are called, at the national archives at Kew, the cabinet notebooks. In physical appearance, the notebooks – those that counsel has seen, at least – are large soft-backed exercise books of lined pages; the one in question, designated CAB 195/2 is filled with the small, neat handwriting of the then deputy cabinet secretary, Norman Brook. He was evidently not a shorthand writer and he used a simple, rather primitive system of abbreviations to record what was being said and by whom. The effect is terse and staccato and we can be sure that this august civil servant did not have in mind that his jottings might one day be spread before a wide public; he was simply making the first draft of a summary of proceedings. Not all of it is intelligible to us nowadays but nonetheless it gives a glimpse, a fuzzy snapshot perhaps, of the cabinet's collective reaction. Of even greater interest, members of the jury, if you are able to go online and surf as you please, you may visit the typed transcript of these records (the original is deemed too fragile for casual inspection) by copying this link:

www.nationalarchives.gov.uk/documents/cab_195_2_transcript.pdf

The notebook versions are, for any historian, gold dust albeit very much in the raw; they record the rows, the conflict, the lunging and jibing of ministerial difference and sometimes expose the authentic political calculations thrown up by events. At this time, the spring of 1943, the ebb and flow of war news of course dominates; the Burma campaign, the war on the eastern front; the battle of the Atlantic; at home, war production, food supply, casualty figures from the air raids.

So it was with the shelter disaster, which occurs at two points in the notebooks. The first exchange on March 8, five days after the event, was chaired by Sir Anthony Eden. This was the laconic, handwritten summary recorded by Norman Brook (the initials HO stand for Morrison, home office and ministry of home security; LP the Lord President, Sir John Anderson, MAP was Cripps and AE was Eden, MI was Minister for Information); here is Morrison reporting, as heard by Norman Brook:

*H.O: Bethnal Green shelter. Soon after alert on Wed. evening. Total killed 180. Announcemt. held up for some hours: stress factual statement released after consultation with P.M. & M/I. Have seen the two M.P.s & the mayor. People in the vicinity are worried – mtg. at Oxford House on Sat. p.m. Read letter fr. Percy Harris M.P. who attended the mtg. Mtg wanted immediate public enquiry under a judge: Harris said I was ready to accede to such a request. Think there ought to be inquiry, conducted by an impartial person. Pro public inquiry: matter of public interest. Wd. have a re-assuring effect. public demand locally & in press. Pro private inquiry: security ques may be raised with published findings: effect on public morale of continued publicity. opportunity for propaganda by disaffected local people. war conditions are difft. from peace. Favour private inquiry by Dunne, Met. Mag.*

*Statement in H/C or in press: Tuesday or Wed. Read draft statement.*

*L.P. Clearly shd not be held in public? Worth while associating assessors with Met. Mag.*

*H.O. Considered that : but against it. They can be called as witnesses. M.A.P. Public assocn of Met. Mag. with Met. Police.*

*H.O. My reason was public realise Met. Mags. know London.*

*A.E. Announce in House if possible. Agreed.*

**Morrison: "Parliamentary resposibility undoubtedly mine"**

Clearly the cabinet immediately balked at bringing the matter into the open and went along, perhaps hesitantly, with Morrison's intention to have the investigation carried out by someone more amenable to Whitehall pressure, and with less political weight than a judge. Already they could foresee that the report's conclusions might need to be kept from the public. Having taken the temperature in the cabinet, the minister went to the House of Commons forty-eight hours later to make a statement and face the questions. Here (extracted from Hansard, the official record) is most of what he said:

"While a number of people were moving quickly down these stairs to the shelter a woman fell and this caused the fall of a number of those behind her, thus causing a stoppage which, through the unintentional pressure of the crowd from above, quickly grew into a tangled mass of people who could not release themselves or be extricated for some time. As a result, 173 persons lost their lives and 61 were injured and removed to hospital. The government are determined to do whatever is possible to throw light upon the circumstances attending this sad event. Without in any way assuming that there was negligence in any quarter, the government wish to be assured, and wish the public to be assured, that any avoidable defect either in the structure and equipment of the shelter, or in the arrangements for its staffing, or for the supervision of those within the shelter, is brought to light so that steps can be taken both in this shelter and elsewhere to minimise the risk of any repetition."

Mr Morrison announced the appointment of Mr Dunne and added: "As many aspects of the incident concern civil defence arrangements related to acts of war, on which it is undesirable that information should be given to the enemy, the government have decided that the inquiry should be held in private; but the conclusions will, subject to security considerations, be published".

Questions then followed ...

Mr Thorne: "May I take it that one of the questions that will be inquired into is whether that shelter and other shelters are properly lighted?" Mr Morrison: "Yes, sir".

Sir Percy Harris: "Will special facilities be given for the relatives of those who suffered in this appalling disaster to give evidence, and will counsel be employed, or what is the procedure likely to be?"

Mr Morrison: "As the right hon. gentleman will appreciate, the determination as to procedure and witnesses must rest with Mr. Dunne. I should doubt whether this matter is of a nature in which counsel could assist in the inquiry. With regard to witnesses, that matter will be within the discretion of Mr. Dunne, but I should have thought the material witnesses would be the persons who are concerned with the administration of the shelter and persons who were present".

Colonel Sir Charles MacAndrew: "In view of the fact that there are rumours that certain persons shouted that they saw bombs falling, and encouraged a stampede, has the right hon. gentleman sufficient power to deal with such scoundrels at present?"

Mr Morrison: "If these were malicious statements, we certainly should have powers to deal with them".

Mr Frankel: "Would it not be possible for part of the inquiry to be held in public, even if some of the things alleged in the public part were repressed in order not to allow the enemy to hear anything which, in the opinion of the home secretary, he should not be allowed to hear?"

Mr Morrison: "I have considered that point. Naturally it is exceedingly difficult to draw an arbitrary line as to what is security and what is not, and there is also the point that you cannot be sure of what a witness is going to say when he is in the middle of saying it."

Mr Maxton: "Whose is the responsibility of seeing that tragic accidents of this kind do not occur? Does it rest with the local authorities, the regional commissioner, the Metropolitan Police or the home secretary?"

Mr Morrison: "The Parliamentary responsibility is undoubtedly fully mine, and I accept it. The local responsibility is primarily that of the local authority, in association with the regional commissioner."

Sir Irving Albery: "Is the right hon. gentleman aware that, even under peace-time conditions, many of the stairways leading into the tubes are definitely dangerous, if they have to be used owing to failure of the lifts, unless there is adequate control, and will this also be inquired into?"

Mr Morrison: "I am afraid I have not enough knowledge of all tube stairways to answer that question but this is not a point that would be inquired into. Only the accident at this shelter will be inquired into. But, if anything comes out which would be applicable to other tube stations, no doubt the minister of war transport would consider any general steps which might be desirable."

Sir H Williams: "As the inquiry is to be conducted by one person and held in secret, will arrangements be made for some representatives of the local authority to be present throughout the proceedings? Of course, I am not making any reflection on Mr. Dunne."

Mr Morrison: "I should not like to give a firm answer. It is a matter within the discretion of Mr. Dunne. If he wishes to have the local authority people present all the time, he can do so. The local authorities, the regional commissioners and myself are potential subjects of criticism, and that point must be kept in mind."

Sir H Williams: "Is it desirable that a secret inquiry should be conducted with no one present except the person conducting the inquiry and those whose evidence is being heard?"

Mr Morrison: "There is no difficulty whatever in Mr. Dunne having any assistance he wishes, and I have no doubt he will require assistance of various sorts, and that point will be in his mind."

Mr Chater: "I should like to be assured that this inquiry in private, in view of the very wild statements and the blame that has been laid in the locality on persons likely to be proved not blameworthy, will give a full opportunity for those persons to be exculpated from all blame."

Mr Morrison: "The point my hon. friend is putting is whether it is fair to the authorities who are normally responsible for the administration of the shelter, and there is point in that. I have given the matter very careful consideration, and, while in peace-time I would not hesitate at all that this inquiry should be public, we are at war, and there are lessons not only for ourselves but for the enemy in the tactics he uses against us. I am sure that in the public interest this inquiry must be held in private, although, as I have said, the conclusions, subject to security considerations, will be published."

Members of the jury, Dan Chater was one of the Bethnal Green MPs and we can allow ourselves to suspect from this last passage that he was attempting to warn the minister that the councillors of Bethnal Green should not be set up as negligent or blameworthy. As we shall see, Mr Chater and others were soon lost in the fog of 'national security' that was about to roll out of Whitehall.

The second of the two Cabinet discussions on the Bethnal Green tragedy came a month later, on April 5, and included the ministerial summary of Mr Dunne's report. In the light of what has gone before, the jury may wonder if this is another example of the fabled ministerial ability to 'spin'. Here is the document that was seen by the cabinet before they spoke:

W.P. (43) 137
April 3, 1943.

TO BE KEPT UNDER LOCK AND KEY
It is requested that special care may be taken to
ensure the secrecy of this document

WAR CABINET.

-------------

TUBE SHELTER INQUIRY
REPORT BY MR. DUNNE.

MEMORANDUM BY THE HOME SECRETARY
AND MINISTER OF HOME SECURITY

1. I have already circulated to the Civil Defence Committee
(C.D.C. (43) 10) copies of Mr. Dunne's report on the London Tube
Shelter disaster.
2. I stated in the House of Commons on the 10th March that,
subject to security considerations, Mr. Dunne's conclusions would
be published.
3. The report — a document of 63 paragraphs — is in narrative
form, without any summary of conclusions. These emerge
cumulatively from reading the text. Mr. Dunne does however end
his report with the following "two short propositions."
" (a) this disaster was caused by a number of people losing
their self-control at a particularly unfortunate place and time;
(b) no forethought in the matter of structural design or
practicable police supervision can be any real safeguard against
the effects of a loss of self-control by a crowd. The surest
protection must always be that self-control and practical common
sense the display of which has hitherto prevented the people of
this country being the victims of countless similar disasters."
4. Earlier in his report Mr. Dunne says that the main and
proximate cause of the disaster was a forward surge at the shelter
entrance by probably 350-400 persons who had been considerably
alarmed by the discharge of a salvo of anti-aircraft rockets.
There are other references to loss of self-control, e.g., though
panic is not perhaps the right word, there is no doubt that the
crowd remaining outside the shelter were out of hand and frantic
with nervousness, confusion and worry, which heavier gunfire, and
further salvos of rockets, did nothing to allay."

5. Public reference to the psychological causes of the disaster would, in my view, be likely to assist the enemy. I am not much concerned with the propaganda value to him of passages of the report which could he distorted in an attempt to show that London can no longer "take it." My apprehension is that full knowledge of what happened after the alert on March 3 might tempt the enemy to make further raids on London (possibly quite small nuisance raids) where he must know that there are many tube shelters with restricted means of entrance, in the hope of creating a disproportionate disturbance and loss of life.

6. With a view to meeting these security considerations I have had a summary prepared for publication, modifying the statements in regard to the psychological causes of the disaster, but in no way modifying criticisms of errors of commission or omission in administration. This summary has been agreed by Mr. Dunne. It is embodied in the White Paper, of which a draft is attached.

7. The omission on security grounds of the main and proximate cause of the disaster disturbs the balance of the report and therefore prejudices those responsible for the administration of the shelter in their defence against criticism induced by the publication of Mr. Dunne 's conclusions. I have tried to correct this by sending a copy of the full text of the report to the emergency committee of the local authority concerned for their secret and confidential information. But their public defence of their administration and any public statement which I make on the subject must be restricted to matters which appear in the white paper. H. M.

Home Office, April 3.. 1943.

How energetically Mr Morrison promotes "the main and proximate cause of the disaster." He is alluding, of course, to the "psychological" explanation, the crowd that is "out of hand and frantic with nervousness, confusion and worry". That was a shabby perversion of the reality and it sits uneasily with what the minister said to Londoners just after the tragedy – "Shocking as this blow is, it falls upon a people tested and hardened by the experiences of the blitz and as well able to bear suffering and loss bravely as any people in the world".

That was just political froth of course; but to re-examine the assertions of the cabinet summary, where can we find any evidence of a loss of self control? The police have not supported it; the survivors denied it. And of course, a full and truthful account of the situation must have produced an admission that such an outcome had been foreseen by the people best placed to know, the councillors and employees of the Bethnal Green local authority. But the only references to the council are to imply that, if the truth came out it would have to defend itself against criticism and that only the authorised version from the ministry, woven into the white paper, could be allowed.

Note also Mr Morrison's assertion that "full knowledge of what happened after the alert might tempt the enemy to make further raids on London (possibly quite small nuisance raids)". Nuisance raids, members of the jury? Was that what this was all about? And however obsessed with such a project the enemy might notionally become, the conditions at Bethnal Green tube could not be recreated elsewhere.

So much for Mr Morrison's cabinet memo; let us now turn to the cabinet secretary's transcript of how ministers reacted. They have seen the summary of the white paper, which includes a brisk account of the civil defence refusal to improve the entry to the staircase, but somehow contrives to blame the council for this. As for the "panic" they are not shown the survivors' testimony.

This second cabinet meeting was chaired by Churchill himself. Notice that Sir Kingsley Wood, the chancellor, immediately pounces upon the disclosure that Bethnal Green council had much earlier forecast a potential danger. He remarks that "this situation was envisaged".

Mr Morrison introduces his notion of a psychological aspect behind the accident and discloses that Mr Dunne's findings have been rearranged, explaining – "We have therefore altered Mr Dunne's language". Note the inference behind his acknowledgment that "I can't use this report to protect the government" – an unambiguous signal to his listeners that something needs to be concealed and that full publication would hurt the administration. Here anyway is what Norman Brook recorded on that April day in 1943:

*Tube shelter inquiry.*
*H.O. Two aspects - physical & psychological. The more we stress the second, the greater the security risk. We have therefore altered Mr. Dunne's language: but he agrees fair picture of all that mustn't be withheld on security grounds. Agreed to publish findings so far as security allowed.*

*K.W. Page six shows this situation was envisaged.*

*H.O. I can't use this rpt. to protect govt.*

*P.M. Against giving such limelight to this incident. Flaunting weakest feature. What notice taken of all who died in air attack. Disproportionate importance - meat & drink to enemy & invitation to repeat. Say [report] received & considered: no need to publish: all its lessons are being vigorously applied.*

*Why publish? - Govt.'s position is unassailable. Moreover we said earlier "no panic": this makes it clear there was panic & it was part cause: & this we are withholding.*

*H.O. 170 people killed: shook the public: had to hold inquiry: agitation v. its being private: resisted tht., saying rpt. wd. be published: will be told now that we've something to hide.*

*M/Inf. Short statement in (the House) is equal to publication.*

*H.O. We held off the discontented locals by promise to publish results.*

*P.M. But you are concealing the truth – panic.*

*M.A.P. Say "measures suggested in course of inquiry; defects disclosed & these are being remedied".*

*S/Doms. Make it clear that panic was not due to jews and/or fascists.*

*H.O. undertook to consider.*

Notice, members of the jury, the characteristically robust remarks of Churchill himself – "This makes it clear there was panic" and "why publish? The government's position is unassailable". The 'psychology' notion has had its effect. It could now be argued (in strict secrecy of course) that here was proof that the morale of Londoners might be cracking. In fact it was not, quite the reverse, but it showed the cabinet a way out, a chance to justify suppressing the report. As the prime minister said, the contents of Mr Dunne's report would be "meat and drink to the enemy".

Of course, members of the jury, none of these top-secret calculations leaked into the public domain; the man in the street was left completely in the dark; he was not even supposed to know where the shelter accident had taken place. But Bethnal Green council. understandably dismayed at the obsession with secrecy, wrote to Mr Morrison complaining that what the minister had said in the Commons would lead "to a conclusion that the council cannot be excluded from some considerable degree of blame". They'd seen the Dunne report, they said, and considered themselves exonerated. They were "unaware of any reason why the interests of public security should necessitate the suppression of information which would satisfy the public as to the council's freedom from blame".

Stanley Ferdinando, the town clerk asked for a further ministerial statement vindicating the council and hinted that if it did not materialise, the councillors might issue a statement to that effect. This brought a magisterial reply, signed by a senior official, Sir Oswald Allen, ending with these words: "Any direct or indirect disclosure of the unpublished contents of the report would not only involve a breach of faith with Mr Dunne but could hardly fail to constitute an offence against the provisions of section two of the Official Secrets Act, 1911. The file [HO 205/28] includes an approving handwritten note from Mr Morrison that "this seems an excellent letter and meets squarely all the council's points." The council, loyal, baffled, frustrated, fell silent.

# CHAPTER 4
## Panic? What panic?

Members of the jury we have been reminding ourselves of the gulf between the political calculations that drove the titans of Downing street and Whitehall on the one hand, and the humbler preoccupations of the mortals of the east end. Those people, living near to the heart of the capital, had willy-nilly become part of the front line of aerial attack. Their danger (from the malignant and irrational furies unleashed from Berlin) was not so very much less than soldiers on active service; their stoicism, publicly acclaimed, seems rather to have earned them the silent dislike of Whitehall. Look closer at the cabinet's glad embrace of the "psychology" notion, and you may see that here was a lie for merely political expediency, an ignoble invention, that the English people had become feverish and cowardly, when the truth was, as we have seen, that in the hour of London's peril, they - the people of the East End and elsewhere – remained stolid and dignified.

We've seen what Superintendent Hill had to say about panic. Here's another senior police officer, Inspector Hunt of H division who deals with the notion, propagated to the cabinet by Mr Morrison, that people outside the shelter were 'frantic with worry'.

Respectfully, he differed when Mr Dunne suggested that other police officers "reported to you that they had some very bad trouble when they first arrived there, with the crowd being out of hand and trying to get down into the shelter"?

Insp. Hunt replied: "I believe the statements you have at the moment show that the first officer to arrive did encounter trouble at the entrance, but there are later statements, either on the way to you or of which you are already in possession, which rather discount that."

Q. There was not really any physical interference with the police? A. Apparently not. There was an officer there who was off duty who it now appears was the first officer to arrive on the scene and his statement is on the way to you now.

Q. Has it ever occurred to you that the approach was very vulnerable to being rushed by a crowd? A. Not in this particular case. It has occurred to me and to other senior officers that there might be a danger of rushing at shelters generally, but that was prior to the blitz in the autumn of 1940; it has never occurred to us since.

Q. You never actually had a case of rushing? A. No, sir.

Q. And so the apprehension died down? A. We were all afraid of it before we had raids and then the fear disappeared.

Q. Then it never happened and it seemed unlikely to happen? A. Yes, sir.

Q. There is no doubt, of course, that this really took place? The major trouble here took place because there was a rush into the mouth of this tube shelter?

A. I am not sure, sir. It would only be an opinion. I am not sure that it was. I think that six people could stand on one stair and there were thirteen stairs full of people; that people could enter the shelter at least at the rate of one hundred a minute in the normal way and that a pile of three hundred people could form in two or two-and-a-half minutes.

Q. You think it might have happened without a rush? A. Yes, sir. I have seen similar things at football matches and at railway stations, though not resulting in fatal casualties.

Not much evidence there, you may think, of blind panic. And let us go back to that remark of Mr Dunne's, that there had been bad trouble at the entrance when police arrived. The inquest report elsewhere in this volume and contemporary press accounts can explain that. Among the people at the entrance and waiting, with his wife and others, to enter was an off-duty police constable, Thomas Penn of J division.

When it became clear to the people outside the shelter that something was amiss, constable Penn forced his way through the crowd and struggled across the top of the trapped people below to find out what had gone wrong and, if possible, to do something about it. . He saw the hopeless situation and then struggled back, again over the heads of the mass of people and into the street to send for help. He was in plain clothes and some misunderstood his intentions as he headed downwards; they thought he was a civilian simply trying to jump the queue and get to safety inside the shelter. There were, it seems, angry shouts of 'coward' which died away when he struggled back. This little episode also reinforces the impression that here was an orderly, disciplined crowd, anxious, impatient, but stolidly purposeful too. That was the 'bad trouble' that Mr Dunne had conjectured and which was so assiduously propagated.

Here now is another account of those shelterers entering the staircase from Mr William Lawson, husband and father of two, who lived in Roman Road, Bethnal Green. He told Mr Dunne that he and his wife and children were on their way to the shelter when the sirens started up. He was leading his son, Tony, aged seven, by the hand and in his arms was his daughter Patricia, aged two. Mrs Lawson was carrying clothes and food the family would need for the coming night.

Mr Lawson told the magistrate that when they arrived at the shelter "the people were about six deep, or rather there were six lines of people about three deep at the entrance and they were moving in".

Q. There was no disorder, everybody was going in quietly? A. There was no pushing or rushing about, or fighting or anything like that. It was a bit pushy, not panicky.

Q. When you got inside, how far down did you get? A. I began to go down the steps and I was about four or five steps from the bottom of the first flight. I was not taking a lot of notice of anything that was happening in front of me because the people seemed to be moving down and, of course, I had my baby in my arms and my boy was hanging on to my hand and the wife was a little bit to the side of me and as I got to the spot where I actually stopped, there seemed to be something in front which actually stopped the crowd. There was the warden, the marshal, you know, and about, I should say, four or five men at the bottom of this first set of steps, in that kind of square space before you get to the escalators, on that landing, and they seemed to be holding the crowd back. There were people shouting "all right, let's get on'.

Q. You thought they were holding the crowd back? A. They were definitely holding them back because the crowd was trying to slide round the corner on the right hand side going down [but then] the crowd just stopped dead and they all seemed to be jammed in a straight line. It was definitely a straight line of people who were jammed on that bottom step or just over the bottom step, but there was still that big square space. Of course, the people behind them started pushing and it was terrific, the pushing, and the crowd kind of swayed over that way and I was half-turned and as the crush came I had my baby in my arms and I tried to lift baby up, but of course I got jammed; as I was facing the steps like this (demonstrates) downwards I got jammed this way and I was being held over like this.

Well the crowd behind got more crushed up, and something happened outside. There was a rocket gun or something. I heard it going off myself and some girls started screaming and then all the girls there started screaming and within a matter of about, I should say, ten minutes, five minutes, it could not have been very long, people began to pass out, they began to throw their heads back and flop over.

Nobody fell down because you could not fall down; it was impossible to fall down. At the bottom of these steps there were these men and this warden and I saw the people dying and my little boy was crushed into me and I could only feel his head - and the baby - I could just see her face and I could see she was trying to breathe, because there were other people crushed against me and I was trying to lift her out of my arms and to lift her up above, but I just could not do it, my arms were jammed in and I could not move them an inch.

The people round me were going blue in the face and they were all flopping and they were all going out, kind of dying. Well I began to get scared for the baby's sake and I kept on trying to push her up and hand her to the people down below and I started shouting at this warden fellow, he was only a little way away from me, and I started shouting at him to shift the people in front. If he could only have pulled those people away - I was shouting to him "please pull them away, my baby is dying"; those were the words I was shouting, "my baby is going" , well he did not seem to catch on. He was just shining his torch and he did not seem to know what he was doing; in fact, that was how I took it, with everybody yelling.

And then, of course I began to feel rotten myself, I began to feel as if I was getting crushed and I just could not breathe properly ... I knew the baby had gone, I felt her temple and the pulse in her temple had stopped... I could just see the wife on one side of me and she was being overcome, her head was going back, and my little boy, he was still on his feet and standing up to my hip ... (the witness breaks down) ... well we were like that until the police at the back - it was the police because one person in particular, I will mention this, was shouting from the top, as that chap was shining his torch up and ... of course all the people were dead round me and I was standing on my own then, there was nobody round me, I could see they were dead or they were gone out and as this warden shone his torch up on the crowd they were all lying over or standing up with their heads thrown back, like this, and a soldier fellow from the back of the crowd jumped on top of people's heads and just calmly crawled over the top of them although they were all standing and he jumped down to the front. His object was, I could see his object, to pull the people into this spare space. It seemed so silly you see that all those people should be blocking this front line when there was this big clear piece of space with those men standing there.

They could have - I am sure if I had been there - I would have taken some action and pulled these people from the front to ease the pressure. That is what that fellow tried to do. He was a soldier chap who came from the back as the doors at the back came open. I do not know if they were broken open but there was a hell of a noise up there and then the police began to pull the people away from the very back and as they eased the pressure from the back the people who were leaning this way but still on their feet began to slump down.

Q. That must have been a great deal later, was it not? A. No. There was not such a long wait in between or it did not seem such a long wait

Copy of memorandum by Regional Technical Adviser

BETH/36
RTA/BETH. T.S./AC.

G. BRANCH

### Bethnal Green Tube Station Shelter

#### Construction of an enclosure wall round the entrance

Reference letter, dated the 20th August, from the Town Clerk to the Chief Administrator, I have inspected the site and do not think that a permanent wall of this nature is required here. I also understand from the London Passenger Transport Board that this wall is not required by them and could only be retained for the war. Under the circumstances I think that the present hoarding may be allowed to remain. If the Council are at all nervous about the strength of the hoarding, it might be strengthened by means of salvaged timber.

*Regional Technical Adviser.*

15th September, 1941.

p60

in between the time - or course, the warning was still on and the gunfire was still going.

Q. Did you get out before the all clear? Yes, I was out and I was up at the hospital just before the all-clear went. Of course as the police were pulling the people away and as they dropped around me I was still on my feet and I thought that somehow I might still be able to get some life into the kiddies; I had the baby in my arms and Tony was at my side...

Q. I am terribly sorry. Did your wife come through all right? - A. Yes. She fainted. Well, I will tell you I had no concern for anybody else, only for my own. After that, the police made an opening and everybody was -they were not worrying about how they were pulling them out, they were just walking on the people, and I had the baby in my arms and I handed the baby over to the police. Of course, the police were only concerned with those that were actually alive or had some life left in them and I simply threw the baby over to a policeman and I tried to drag the boy up. The people all fell round him and he was up to his neck in bodies although he was still on his feet, and I just pulled them to one side. I was jammed, my own legs were jammed, but I got him up and I handed him to someone. Of course, I was yelling and shouting and making myself heard. The rescue work was going on, but, to tell you the truth, I was only thinking of them and the wife; I saw her fall on the floor and I managed to get my legs up, out of the people. They were all dead there and by pressing down I managed to get my legs out and I got hold of her in the jam and I walked, I kind of walked on a few people, but I got her outside and, of course, there were a lot of people lying around on the floor and there was a car nearby, I do not know whether it was a police car or what it was, but I know that when I came out with my two children and the wife I put them in the car myself and I got into the car and I told the chap to drive to the hospital, just as if I was a policeman, and he said "I cannot do that just yet". I said "Go on, you just drive to the hospital, I want to save their lives" and I tried some artificial respiration on the kiddies, but it was no good. But they could have been saved if those people in the front who were free and walking about in that square space, I do not only say that mine could have been saved, but the people who did go beforehand, if the pressure could have been eased by just taking the front people away, because the back door was shut; everybody that was taken away would have eased the pressure, but it cannot be actually explained unless you have experienced it.

Q. Tell me about the entrance to the shelter, did you go down there often? - A. Not every night unless there was a raid, say, on Berlin and the wife would think we ought to go.

Q. On some special occasion you would feel you would take the children there? A. She would have the feeling "There might be a raid tonight, we'll go down there".

Q. Did you ever notice that the entrance was dangerous in any way? A. Well it was; it could not be called 'up to the mark' because you could not see your way down.

Q. It was the light? A. There was no light in there of course and you had to be very careful when you went in, you had to be cautious with the kiddies; you could not just simply walk in and walk down. Even with big children you had to pick them up and make sure of your steps.

Mr Lawson's recollections of that night, members of the jury, are grievous and harrowing indeed. But you will note again that there was nothing in his account which supports the 'psychological' theory, of frantic, headlong flight. Too many people were allowed, unchecked, to move through a dark, uneven and confined space and when part of it was accidentally blocked and they lost their footing as, sooner or later was bound to happen, a jam resulted. This was the outcome foreseen, or at least glimpsed, by the shelter committee eighteen months earlier.

Jury you have endured some dreadful stories from the Bethnal Green staircase; shall we close that particular matter with a less painful account, from Mrs Mary Barber, a housewife and mother of five, from 153 Queen street, Russia lane. Amazingly, even though she and her little family were all borne down the stairs and trapped in various positions in the pile of bodies they all survived. At the hearing, ten or so days later, she admitted to Mr Dunne that she was "still a bit shaky".

Q. Are the children all right? A. Yes. The doctor said the eldest one [Mary, aged fourteen] should go to work. She was sitting at home brooding over it.

Q. You have seen to that? A. Yes. The children are going away for a fortnight's holiday next week.

Q. Just before the alert sounded you had already started to go to the shelter with your family? A. That's right. There's a (broadcast) relay in the building and that gives warning six or seven minutes before the alert sounds. The relay says "stand by for a special announcement" and we know what that means and I started making my way to the tube.

Q. What ages are the children? A. One year, four, eight, ten and fourteen.

Q. When you got there, what was going on outside the entrance? A. We were waiting in the road to take our turn. It seemed like few minutes.

Q. People pretty anxious to get in that night? A. Yes, And there were pretty many in front of us.

Q. Was there a bit of pushing even then? A. Yes.

Q. You eventually found yourself going into the entrance? A. It seemed like the gun opened fire as we now know it was a gun.

Q. Where were you when that gun fired? A. In the road, still behind the crowd. Somebody hollered out something, we don't remember no more, we were flung down the stairs.

Q. How far were you from the shelter entrance when that went off? A. We were still in the road.

Q. That went off, somebody hollered out something? A. Yes, There is a landmine.

Q. You heard that? A. Yes, and that is where trouble started.

Q. There was a general rush towards the shelter? A. The stairway, yes.

Q. And before you knew where you were...? A. We were down the bottom, carried down the bottom. Our feet did not touch the stairs.

Q. How far down were you actually carried, where did you finish up? A. I think the fourth stair from the bottom. My eldest girl was lying on the bottom stair. Her head was on the landing and her leg was on the stairs.

Q. Now somebody is said to have tripped up? A. That's right, yes. I just see the woman on the stairs. She fell with the crowd.

Q. She was being carried down. A. And she tripped.

Q. It is fairly clear in your statement 'When we got to the third step from the bottom of the first lot of steps I saw a woman just in front of me fall down'. A. Yes.

Q. As you got further down, I suppose the pressure got very bad? How long did it take you to get carried down, a matter of...? A. A minute. We all seemed to fall. Everybody seemed to be pushed over and fell.

Q. When did you lose your foothold? Near the top of the steps? A. Yes, our feet did not touch the stairs, as I say.

Q. You were just suspended in mid-air? Your children luckily had their heads free, your head was free? A. Yes.

Q. You don't know how long you were there? A. I was taken to the London Hospital about twenty to twelve that night.

Q. You would have been one of the last out? A. Yes, we were.

Q. In your statement to the police you say 'I distinctly saw the first woman fall and the man on top of her'? A. That is right, yes.

Q. This was the start of the trouble. Until they fell the crowd was tightly packed but was on the move? A. Yes, people had already gone down.

Q. Actually there was a rush going on down the stairs ? A. Yes.

Q. She happened to be in the rush, she falls down, the rush goes on and then of course there is this terrible pile up. Do you think the people generally, your friends and acquaintances, were more alarmed before the start of this raid than previously? A. I have not been down there before

Q. Were you expecting something pretty fierce that night? A. I think we all were.

Q. It rather looks as if people generally over London expected to get something pretty unpleasant that night? Of course you had been reading about all the big things we have been throwing on to Berlin and so forth? A. Yes.

Q. And thought they might have one up their sleeve for us? A. Yes.

Q. What do you feel about deep shelters as compared to things like the Salmon and Ball arches? Would you rather be in the tube shelter? A. No, I never use the shelter myself, not the tube, I have never been down there in my life. We have pretty good shelters where we live.

Q. Why did you go there that night? A. I do not like the barrage and one thing and another.

Q. You thought you would like to be quiet? A. Yes.

Q. Have you always had your children in London? A. No, I was lying in with the baby when they came back from the country, they have been back eleven months now.

Q. Do you think it was wise to have them back? A. I did not have them back but people got writing letters, they could not cope with the food problem.

Q. You would like them out of London if we are going to have any of these sorts of incidents. A. Yes, I think they are better off in the country.

Q. Did they have a good time in the country? A. Yes, I have a young boy, 13, and he would not come with me, he has not been right since he has been home from the country.

Q. A lot of your friends, their children have come home? A. Yes.

Q. . There are a lot more children in the borough? A. Yes.

Q. What sort of shelters have you been using, anderson shelters? A. No, flats, shelters made in the bottom flat.

Mr Dunne: Well, thank you very much. I congratulate you in getting away and all your family too. I congratulate you on your presence of mind in being able to remember what happened so clearly.

# CHAPTER 5
## The Secret Inquest

Members of the jury at this point counsel lays before you a transcript of the other inquiry into the tragedy, the secret inquest that began at nearby Shoreditch coroner's court on March 19, 1943. This report, like the transcripts you have been seeing from the Dunne Inquiry, has never been published and even its existence was generally unknown. It covers ground that Mr Dunne's proceedings did not and it also serves to demonstrate that ordinary administrative systems remained in place and functioned perfectly well in spite of wartime exigencies and political calculations elsewhere.

The coroner was Mr W R H Heddy, an inquest jury was sworn and press and public were excluded. Witnesses were marshalled into the court one by one. This record was compiled by a London police officer, constable Dudley Davies of G Division. It can be found in a file designated MEPO 3/1942 at the national archives at Kew.

Inevitably there is repetition of material arising out of the Dunne inquiry, and so it has been telescoped and, here and there, edited but only for ease of understanding. Counsel suggests that the jury will find it revealing and notable not only for the way in which the coroner sticks firmly to a factual path. Unlike the questioning that witnesses faced at the Dunne inquiry, there was no attempt to establish any kind of theme to this drama. Mr Heddy is emphatic that there was no panic just "a sudden mass fall as it were, and in a moment you had a vast heap of struggling people pinning each other down".

Here is constable Davies' report:

The jury being sworn, the coroner then addressed them as follows: "You know in view of this dreadful disaster that has overtaken the people in this part of the world, an inquiry is proceeding and is expected before long to present its report, and it is common knowledge that the inquiry is concerning itself with every aspect of the disaster, including such questions as the suitability of the premises, the construction of the staircase, the lighting of it, staff arrangements, etc.

"The inquiry will also concern itself with the question of the responsibility with various authorities and also deal with shortcomings attributable to authorities or individuals. That is the nature and purpose of this inquiry. That being the case you may say to yourselves, how comes it that this inquest is necessary at all and why is it called here this morning?

"Dealing with the first point, the necessity for an inquest: An inquest is necessary because certain matters touching the deaths of these poor people can be dealt with by this court and this court alone. Identification, the taking of medical evidence and of sufficient evidence to enable this court to return a verdict – these are all essential points which have to be dealt with, and can only be dealt with in this court. Less than that the court cannot do and more than that it most assuredly is not required to do.

"Now we come to the question of why we are here this morning, and I will frankly tell you that it would have been possible for me, under the administration of justice emergency provisions act, to have sat here this morning and carried out the duty by myself alone; that I should have had power to do so. However I thought it desirable if only you may see that all the matters that have to be dealt with are properly and efficiently dealt with; also I thought it desirable that, as you represent more or less the general public, you should hear at first hand, on oath, the evidence of the witnesses who will be called.

"The scope of your inquiry will be limited and what you have to do, in accordance with the terms of your oath, after having heard the evidence, is to return a verdict as to how, where and by what means these poor people came by their deaths. When you have done that, you will have discharged your duty. Then I will deal with the issue of certificates and so far as this court is concerned, this sad tragedy will be completed.

*Witness Cecil Doughty, police constable, 166, G Division*

Q. Were you present in court when details of identification of 173 victims of the shelter disaster were made? A. I was sir.

Q. Were these identifications carried out in the prescribed form and on oath according to law? A. They were, sir.

Q. Have all these bodies been identified? A. Every one.

Q. The total being one-hundred-and-seventy-three. How exactly is the number constituted?

A. There are: males 28; females 81; children of 16 years and under 64.

Q. There has been a little discrepancy in some of the published figures, and I take it the 16s have been reckoned and the under 16s not reckoned; these figures are accurate and correct? A. If you please sir.

Q. You have a list of the names of the people who have been identified; that is available and we will let the jury have a look? A. Yes sir.

*John Portwood, police constable 687, H Division.*

Q. You have prepared a plan of the scene of this disaster? A. Yes, sir.

Q. Dealing with it very briefly, it shows a straight flight of nineteen steps from the ground level to a landing ten feet by fifteen? A. Yes sir.

Q. What would be the distance from the kerb of the pavement there to the actual commencement of the steps, including the space behind the wooden gates? A. About ten to twelve feet wide there and the distance from the entrance is seven or eight feet to the top of the first steps.

Q. At the top there are three wooden gates extending over the total width of ten feet? A. It is slightly more than that because of the angle.

Q. Did you see this staircase when it was dark? A. There was one light over the seventh step up from the landing sir. It was dimly lit.

Q. In section these nineteen steps are at an angle of about how much? A. There is only a very slight angle.

Q. They are not particularly steep steps? A. Oh no not steep.

Q. The construction of the steps themselves... have they wooden fronts? A. Yes, they are partly finished, everything is rough.

Q. When you saw them, although in the rough, was their general condition good? A. Fairly good.

*Mr. Ernest Reed, local emergency officer, ministry of pensions*

Q. Mr. Reed, has it been decided by the ministry that these poor people's relatives shall rank in exactly the same position as if they had died of war operations? A. Yes sir.

Q. You were able to get the decision from the department the following morning, and it is exactly what it would have been if they had been killed by enemy bombs or one of our own shells? A. Yes sir.

Q. With regard to the administration of pensions, payments have already begun? A. Yes, pensions and war injury allowances.

Q. In regards to injuries, have you any information about the plight of people in hospital?

A. No, sir, we haven't that information. Injury allowances are being paid to people in hospital. And pensions, if permanently injured will be paid later on.

*Mrs Mary Barber, Russia lane, E2*

Q. You arrived at the shelter with five children soon after the alert? A. Yes.

Q. When you got to the shelter, you went in with other people? A. No sir, we were waiting outside.

Q. And then eventually you went down, with your five children. How old were they? A. The eldest is 14, the youngest one year.

Q. Five children, single-handed, and you went down the steps? What was it like? Did you go steadily down? A. Our feet didn't touch the stairs. We were just carried down.

Q. Were you alarmed? A. I wasn't alarmed. I just thought 'we're going down'.

Q. You had one child in your arms? And the other little ones were looked after by the child of fourteen, all close together? A. Yes, all together.

Q. Mrs. Barber, as you got near the bottom of the flight of steps, did you see anything happen? Did you see anybody fall? A. Yes sir, a woman.

Q. Did you see anybody else fall after that? A. We all seemed to fall.

Q. People behind, on top of you, and you fell, with the baby? A. Yes, Mr. Steadman took the baby out of my arms.

Q. When you fell other people fell on top of you? A. Yes.

Q. Did you have your head free? A. Yes sir.

Q. Could you see anything of your children? A. I could just see their hands up.

Q. You could make out all five of them? A. Yes.

Q. Were you about the middle of the staircase? A. I think about fourth step from the bottom.

Q. And then what happened? A. As the police worked the crowd backwards we were released.

Q. How long were you in the actual pile for? A. About three hours. We were taken to the London Hospital about twenty-to-twelve.

Q. All the time you could see your children? A. Yes, sir.

Q, .Did anybody come up and try to get you out? A. Yes sir.

Q. As a matter of fact, it is a thing you haven't told us, you yourself assisted the police to get them out? A. Yes.

Q. You were doing that for some time? A. Yes my legs were caught but I had my body free.

Q. You directed the police officers as to where the children lay and where the people could safely be pulled out from, and eventually you yourself were released, and your children? A. Yes, sir.

Q, All of you released safely, a few cuts and bruises, otherwise all right? A. Yes. Q. That was very fortunate for you, wasn't it? A. Yes.

*Mr. Richard Cotter, 413 Roman road, E2*

Q. Mr Cotter, you were standing at the top of the escalator? A. Yes sir.

Q. The crowd was passing down just in the normal way? A. Very normal.

Q. You have watched the people many times before? A. Yes, sir.

Q. And the crowd continued to pour down the escalator in the ordinary way? A. Yes.

Q. What did you notice? A. I noticed a little thinning out of the crowd and immediately after that a call for help.

Q. What did you do? A. I immediately ran round to where I heard the call, up the first flight of steps on to the landing.

Q. When you got on to the landing, what did you see? A. Just one mass of people on top of one another struggling and a mass coming down the stairs.

Q. Were you alone on the landing? A. There were other people. I tried to drag the bodies off the top, but others were falling and it was impossible to move them. I immediately ran to the telephone for the police.

Q. Where was that? A. On the booking hall.

Q. Did you ring up Bethnal Green? A. No, you have to ring the office downstairs and they communicated with the police station.

Q. And then after that ...? A. I went back but immediately thought of the people on the escalator, and went to the escalator and helped to remove people from there into the tube.

Q. Actually you yourself saved three infants? A. Yes, I managed to extricate them; two were rather hurt.

*Mr James Lowe, Corfield st. E2.*

Q. You are the area shelter warden, and when the warning sounded what did you do? A. I went up to the main entrance to see that it was open.

Q. When you got there, were all the wooden gates completely open? A. Yes sir.

Q: You stood there for a little while. Did you see the people coming in? A. Yes.

Q. How were they coming in, particularly fast? A. A bit fast but very orderly.

Q. Have you seen crowds coming into that shelter on many occasions? A. Yes sir.

Q. And the crowd at that moment was coming in just as before? A. Yes. After a few minutes, I went down to the booking platform to see if there was anybody hanging about, so as to get them down the escalator. People should not hang about the booking hall.

Q. Were people passing on to the escalator quite all right? A. Yes sir.

Q. And then what happened? A. I had been on the booking platform I should think four to five minutes when I heard screams and shouts. I rushed up on to the landing, well, I could see it was quite hopeless because they were piling in on top of one another. The only thing I could do was to stand by and say, 'For god's sake keep back'.

Q., Were there other people with you at the time? A. There were a number of people there, Mr. Cotter and Mr. Steadman.

Q. Did you try to extricate some of these poor people? A. We did have a try, but it was hopeless, sir, because they were interlocked. Well, we could only go downstairs and see if they had sent for the police. They had already so we came up to the top to see what we could do to alleviate the distress of the people crying out.

p71

Q. The police eventually arrived; how soon do you think they arrived?

A. About nine-thirty sir, at the bottom; I couldn't say what was going on outside, sir.

*Mrs. Matilda Crabb, Whitman house, Roman road, E.2.*

Q. At about eight-twenty-five on that evening did you leave your flat with your son Sidney to go to the shelter; he is a lad of 18? A. Yes, sir.

Q. When you arrived at the shelter about ten minutes after the warning had gone, what was the state of affairs? A. There was a tremendous crowd stretching from the shelter entrance to the kerb.

Q. Did it overflow from the kerb? A, Not when I was there.

Q. What was the state of affairs overhead? A. Guns were going at the time rather heavily, and there seemed to be a rocket going in the air.

Q. This crowd was just standing still, quite orderly, to see if it could get into the shelter? No panic? No stampeding? Crowd standing, trying to see if it could get into the shelter? A. Yes.

Q. You got into the crowd. Was there any movement either way? A. None whatever. We stood there a little while and when there wasn't any chance of getting in, we walked along home.

Q. You thought it might move and you would get in; actually it didn't move? A. No

Q. While you were in the crowd you were not jostled or upset, or pushed about? You could not make any movement; just a crowd standing there, a static crowd? A. Yes.

*Mrs. Ivy Ada Peel, Butler estate, Roman road. E2*

Q. Did you arrive at the shelter about ten minutes after the alert had gone? A. Yes.

Q. Was there a large crowd? A. Yes sir, a large crowd.

Q. Did the crowd seem to be moving? A. Yes.

Q. Was the crowd orderly? A. They were in a hurry.

Q. And at that time was there a little extra noise in the sky? A. Yes sir.

Q. Did that have any effect on things? A. It made people push rather.

Q. And did you succeed in getting into the shelter, on to the staircase? A. Not on to the staircase. About a yard from the top.

Q. And then what happened? A. I was just stuck.

Q. Could you see down the staircase at all? A. No.

Q. Did any of the people seem to be seeing down the staircase? A. No.

Q. How long do you think you were there? A. I should think ten minutes.

Q. While you were standing there were you crushed at all? Pretty uncomfortable? A. Yes.

Q. Then what happened? A. We seemed to be loosening from the back, and I gradually got out of the crowd and into the street.

Q. You didn't realise, Mrs. Peel, what had in fact happened down below? A. No.

Q Did other people realise? A. Not around me. Other people might. I didn't think the crowd was so great; I couldn't see..

*Mrs. Rose Lewis, Whitman House, Roman road, E.2*

Q. About ten minutes after the alert, were you making your way to the shelter? A. Yes sir

Q. When you arrived, did you see a crowd? Were they moving? A. They were just beginning to about that time.

Q. When you first arrived they were making their way in, and as you got there they seemed to be stopped; was the crowd orderly? A. Very orderly.

Q. And as you approached the gate, was there any difference in the noises outside, any alteration in what was happening? A. There wasn't any alteration in the crowd; they were beginning to wonder why they couldn't get in.

Q. How near did you get to the shelter? A. Just by the kerb. I heard some people beginning to call out why they couldn't get in: 'Get a move on'; 'door shut again' and different things.

Q. You didn't know what had happened down below? A. No.

Q. Do you think from the remarks, they had any idea of what had happened? A. No. sir.

Q. You didn't hear anybody wanting to rush in? A. They were beginning to get touchy after a time because they heard cries and noises from the shelter and people outside got worried about people going in. My daughter... I thought she was there, but she was at the top on the outside.

Q. After a few moments, did the police arrive with home guards?

A. Some little time after. Evidently they had been sent for and then they came in bulk.

Q. Was the crowd then dispersed? A. Some moved away almost immediately; others waited to see what had gone wrong and were calling out for relatives and friends.

Q. Was it difficult for police and home guard to get people to move? A. Not a great deal of difficulty.

Q. Did you see any panic, rush or stampede of people? A. There were a few people hurrying from the buildings.They may have broken into a run?

*Thomas Penn, P.C. 322 J Div*

Q. On this night in question, at the time the warning went, you were off duty? A. Yes sir.

Q. And did you proceed to the shelter when the alert went? A. Yes sir

Q. Who went with you to the shelter? A. My wife and young son, three years of age, and mother in law, and brother in law who is in the army.

Q. You were in plain clothes? A. Yes, I was wearing a lumber jacket, scarf and overcoat. My wife was carrying my steel helmet.

Q. When you got to the shelter, what was the state of affairs? A. The entrance appeared to be crowded with people trying to get down into the shelter.

Q. Did the crowd at that time seem to be moving? A. Slightly, and then moved back. They didn't appear to be getting in.

Q. You saw a police officer there trying to deal with the crowd? A. Yes.

Q. Did you ask him if you could give him a hand? A. I endeavoured to get to him but couldn't so I got as near as I could and shouted to him.

Q. You sent the wife and family away, feeling it was hopeless to get into the shelter? A. Yes.

Q. Then did you push your way through the crowd? A. Yes.

Q. How far did you get on the first occasion before you sent the wife and children away?

A: Somewhere near the top of the stairs leading down.. I was in the midst of a number of people and there was a deal of shouting about 'open the doors', 'put the light out', and in order to ascertain the cause

I got on top of the people and went down to the base of the shelter landing.

Q. You made your way, scrambling over the top, right down to the landing; and as you went over, you could see there was a terrible crush? A. Yes, sir.

O. When you got to the landing, could you speak to the people below? A. I could see what was the matter and spoke to one man who had a large torch and asked him to be careful as the torch was making people at the top a little more excited.

Q. You thought the flashes of light would upset the crowd still more? A. Yes sir.

Q. When you arrived and climbed over this pile of people, and got into touch with the people on the landing, what was happening? Did they seem to be trying to extricate people?

A. A number of men were there and they didn't have much success and I decided to go back the way I had come and get assistance from police if possible.

Q. You crawled back over this mass of people and when you got to the top did you have difficulty in getting through the crowd? A. Not so much.

Q. Did you catch hold of somebody to take a message? A. Yes, a lad of sixteen or seventeen, I sent him to the police station to tell them to send as much assistance as possible.

Q. And then what did you do? A. I shouted to the police officer but he didn't let on he'd heard me, and then I circulated among the crowd and told them it was impossible to get into the shelter and they should to go to the air-raid shelter in the arches. The crowd loosened quite a lot.

Q. Then what did you do? A. Well, I assisted removing injured people and by this time there were quite a number working from the top and there was a lot of shouting from the bottom, and they appeared to be getting a bit excited, so I went down the stairs again. We tried to organise some means of getting people out.

Q. With regard to getting people out, could you get any idea of what was being done? A. We were unable to do anything at that time. Some people took me and gave me a seat and I had some water and went back. Once again we endeavoured to get people out, without success.

Q. And then did you go to the bottom of the escalator? A. No, sir, I went away again and felt faint and people took me to the bottom of the escalator, and I received medical attention from the shelter nurse. I stopped in the medical ward of the shelter, and then bodies were being removed and I assisted to the best of my ability in carrying them down the stairs.

Q. By this time police officers had arrived in large numbers? Now the people were being got out? A. Yes.

Q. You walked right through to the other exit of the tube? A. Yes.

Q. You didn't feel like going up the staircase again? A. No.

Coroner: You seem to have behaved in a very praiseworthy manner.

*Mr. Percival James Bridger, Stewart Headlam School, Summerford street, Bethnal Green.*

Q. You are a school teacher employed by the borough council and chief warden of this shelter; how long have you known this shelter? A. Since it was opened in October 1940.

Q. What is your estimate of the capacity of the shelter? A. There is bunking space for five-thousand and on top of that it can take another five-thousand.

Q. Casting your mind back to the days of 1940 and the spring of 1941, what sort of numbers did you have in the shelter then? A. The figure ranged between three-thousand-five-hundred and six-thousand.

Q. Have you experienced any difficulty in regard to any particular aspect of the shelter? Has there been any particular trouble?

A. No, the shelter always ran very smoothly. There were large numbers and we got them in fairly early.

Q. On occasions you have had large numbers of people in, in a very short space of time? A. Yes.

Q. Thinking of short, sharp raids? A. Yes.

Q. Has there to your knowledge ever been any serious accident on the staircase? A. One or two minor cases, that's all.

Q. On the night in question, did you arrive at about 8.22 at the shelter? A. I was at the town hall when the warning went and proceeded to the shelter. I walked from the entrance with the people, down the hall to the bottom and to the office.

Q. The people were coming in in large numbers but flowing quite smoothly? A. Yes the escalator itself was packed with people, but they were moving quite smoothly.

Q. Everything was going on as usual. What was the first you knew that there was anything amiss?

A. I received a telephone message on our internal telephone system asking me to send for the police as there was trouble at the top.

Q. Mr Cotter said there was congestion at the top and would you get police help. What did you do? A . I telephoned to the police station immediately. Then there was another message from the top and it was realised that a sudden stoppage had taken place. There was a break in the people coming in, and Mr Cotter came down to me and Mr Hastings went to see what the trouble was. I telephoned to the police again and explained that there was a very serious situation, people trapped and piling up on one another. Until pressure was removed from outside we could do nothing. I asked them to send all available men. I was told police officers had already left. They had sent eight men out at that time.

Q. You went to the foot of the escalator and saw your deputy? A . Yes he met me and explained again what had happened. I telephoned control and asked them to send all available services, ambulances, light rescue services, first aid and so forth, and doctors.

Q. Did you get a satisfactory response from the town hall? A. Yes I checked up by phoning through again to ask what had been done, and how things were going on, because we were helpless to know what was going on outside.

Q. By this time had any police officers arrived by the Carlton square entry? A. A little time after that. It would take some time to get down there.

Q. They had to come through the shelter at the bottom. A. Yes.

Q. Did you arrange for the removal of certain casualties downstairs? A. Yes to the first aid post. Everything was cleared so that the casualties could be taken to the post.

Q. What was the number of wardens on duty between the escalator and the entry? A. Four, two or three would be the normal number; one was sent up extra, one in the booking hall, one at the top of the escalator steps and one at the bottom. The one at the bottom was sent up on the preliminary warning being given.

Q. The question of the staircase construction is not a matter to go into in this court, but just from the point of view of throwing light on the witnesses; this staircase is about ten feet wide? A. Yes.

Q. There were, at that time, no hand rails down the middle, just rails at the side? A. Yes.

*Mr Alfred William Hastings, Swinburne house, Roman road, E2*

Q, You are deputy chief warden at the shelter and a member of Bethnal Green borough council? Before I ask you what happened; tell me something about the light. What was the lighting system?

A. On the principal staircase, consisting of 19 steps, there was an obscured, 25 watt lamp. It had been covered up to conform with regulations.

Q. What was the first you knew on that night? A. I was doing the ordinary duties about the shelter when the bell rang and Mr. Bridger took the message that there was trouble at the top and we sent for the police. Such a message told us nothing and we thought it would just be an ordinary case of someone drunk or obstreperous.

Q. When you got to the top what did you find? A. As soon as I got to the first landing I saw people piled up in a mass to a height of five feet and people piling on top of them, right away back, and pressure coming in from the gates. I ran down the escalator and told them we needed fifty police at the least. When I left the landing there were people trying to extricate these people and three wardens there working like trojans. Police arrived round about nine o'clock. What happened outside, I don't know. Then we had a message from control asking us to open the Carlton Square entrance, but there was no need; they had been been burst open by people from Stepney and at least two-hundred had come in that-way.

Q. Did the services function satisfactorily from your point of view? Did they get to work quickly? A. As far as I can see, they were on the spot, almost immediately; police came in from Carlton Square and gave great service. I have never seen men work better.

*Police sub-divisional inspector Hunt*

Q. Were you informed, at about 8-45 on March 3, by Inspector Ferguson, that he had received a report from Sergeant Swindells that there was trouble at the entrance to the shelter? A. I was.

Q. Had Sergeant Swindells taken any action? A. He had sent every man available, section, a sergeant and fifteen constables. He sent those on his own initiative.

Q. Was the message you received to the effect that the force sent was unable to cope with the situation and that further aid was required? A. That is so. I contacted Bethnal Green station to ascertain precise details and was informed that there was a large number of casualties and a blockage at the entrance to the tube station, and it was advisable to attack it from both ends at once. That is to say from the staircase entrance and the emergency exit at Carlton Square.

Q. When you arrived, what was the situation at the entrance? A. I got there about nine o'clock. There was a lot of people in the entrance, but they were all rescuers or would-be rescuers and helpers. There was no longer people trying to crush their way into the shelter. About a dozen people were lying on stretchers on the footway, and a number of ambulances were being loaded or drawing off and some form of organisation among police, rescue party, home guard and others endeavouring to extricate people from the top of the pile, and some sort of system to carry people up the stairs on to the footway where the stretchers were.

Q. At this time, I take it, there was considerable difficulty experienced in actually extricating people from the top? A. It is difficult to believe how difficult it was to remove people from this pile. It was almost impossible to sort out which person wasn't inextricably fixed into the pile of people.

Q. Did you form any opinion as to what was done in that way? A. At that time I could not understand why people below were not doing more to get them away and I decided to go to control to establish contact with people inside the shelter. I went to the control room at the town hall, about three or four minutes in the car, and telephoned Mr Bridger and told him it was essential to use every effort to remove people from the bottom as it was hopeless to make any attempt from the top to get them out alive.

Q. You carried on with the rescue at the top until 9.45 and then what did you do?

A. They were still not releasing people below and to make thoroughly certain they had understood my request I climbed down over the pile to establish contact with the police party below, and assisted at the bottom until all the casualties had been removed.

Q. What time was it when all the people had been released? A. About half-past eleven.

Q. Were people being removed alive up to that time? A. Almost the last person removed was a girl about seven years old, who walked down to the first aid post unaided.

Q. What was the total strength employed from the division? A. Between sixty and seventy constables and a number of senior officers.

*Dr. Ralph Summers, divisional surgeon*

Q. You were called to the shelter, where was that from? A. I was at Arbour Square police station. I heard there had been some trouble at this shelter and there were a number of casualties.

Q. When you arrived, was there a crowd there? A. Not actually at the entrance; there was a crowd around.

Q. Did you go down the staircase? A. I looked in the staircase and saw a number of police officers and others endeavouring to get people out, and a number of people lying on stretchers. I went to the people on stretchers on the pavement. A large number were dead.

Q. In the difficult circumstances, did you form any opinion then as to the probable cause of death? A. In nearly every case it was due to asphyxia.

Q. Having seen the people in the street did you then have a look at the state of affairs on the staircase? A. As the staircase gradually cleared I ran down into the booking hail and saw a number of people lying on stretchers. There was no question of giving any treatment as they were either dead or alive and reasonably safe.

Q. It really amounts to this; physical injuries were relatively slight? A. There were very few fractured bones.

Q. It is an interesting fact that there were 173 casualties inspected immediately after this occurrence, that is the number we are dealing with, and not one single death has been reported since, which is probably not surprising; directly the pressure was removed they were able to recover. When you got down the stairs and into the booking hall and the deeper parts of the shelter did it seem to you, considering the difficulties, that things were being properly organised? A. They were well organised by the time I got there. Many of the casualties had been taken downstairs. A number were tackled from below and taken deep into the shelter and I saw them down there in the first aid room.

Q. Having before our eyes the dreadful spectacle of this mass of people, two hundred or more, and having regard to the signs that were formed, Dr Summers, you would have no doubt that they died of asphyxia? A. Quite certain, due to compression. The number of injuries, fractured 1imbs and so forth was very small. I don't think I saw a single case of fractured ribs.

*Dr Edwin Jeffrey Minett Palmer, assistant medical officer Bethnal Green hospital*

Q. Did you see sixty-two bodies which were brought to your hospital? A. I saw forty-five, the remaining seventeen were taken direct to the mortuary.

Q. Did you have any casualties from people who were alive when they arrived? A. Twenty-seven.

Q. What were they suffering from? A. Most of them from minor injuries; a great many from bruises and abrasions of the legs, mostly below the knee – quite half of them. Others various minor injuries.

Q. Are all the patients going on well? A. About half of them were discharged the following morning; others were transferred to the hospital at Winchmore hill. Three gave rise to some anxiety at the time but I have heard they have gone on all right.

Q. With regard to the bodies that you saw dead, did you at that time form any opinion as to the cause of death? A. When they were brought in at first, I was under the impression they were air-raid casualties. But on examining them, I found no trace of injuries. They were a little blue and I thought they must have died of asphyxia. It was not until later that I was told they had died because of an accident and not as air-raid casualties.

*Dr. Cedric Keith Simpson, pathologist*

Q. You made post-mortem examinations of four persons who were victims in this disaster and will you first let me have your report on Henry Julier, aged 18? A. In this case, which I examined on the fifth of March, in the afternoon, about forty-three hours after death, I found he had been a healthy subject without natural disease of any kind capable of bearing on the cause of death. There was plain evidence of asphyxia due to very heavy pinning and crushing. From pinning, compression and crushing in this case, it was evident that this pressure was sustained in particular across the left side of the trunk and left thigh. There was a heavy clothing pressure mark to the thigh region and above this level, and very deep-blue suffocation changes in the blood.

There were many haemorrhages showing intense asphyxia changes. Internally there was evidence of heavy sustained compression of the abdomen. The deceased had remained alive for a short time subsequent to being released. In this case the stomach had been distended to a gross degree and the intestines similarly. As regards the hip and thigh injuries, these showed remarkable compression changes in the muscle similar to those I have seen as a result of pinning by baulks of timber in collapsed houses and debris. It was quite clear that the weight was very great indeed that had been sustained. I found during the course of examination minor surface injuries, glancing abrasions to the left forearm, wrist, brow and lips and elsewhere. There was nothing to arouse suspicion of foul play or suggest a scuffle or assault. Death was clearly due to suffocation by compression, by crushing.

Q. You also made the post-mortem examination in the case of Maureen Mead?

A. I made, this examination on the same day and at about the same time and I found the deceased in this case, aged four years, to be a healthy child of good physique and in this case showing very similar injuries to those described, though not quite so heavy. The number of changes which I found consisting of heavy pinning and crushing with the principal weight borne by the left shoulder and chest, the body being bent backward, the head extended upwards and back and the chest bent backward sufficient to snap the ligaments of the vertebral column. In this case there was heavy and sustained pressure. I found, in this case too, quite minor surface injuries - abrasions to the chin running down to the neck, surface bruising of the chest and minor bruising of the lung beneath. I found here nothing to arouse suspicion, the changes being due to sustained compression, death following from asphyxiation from suffocation by compression, due to crushing.

Q. In the case of Antony Lawson and Patricia Lawson, what did you find?

A. In the case of Antony Lawson, I found this child being seven years old, without any natural disease of any kind, of good physical health. In this case there was intense congestion and cyanosis from similar changes but with the maximum compression borne across the chest, the neck, the left of the face, and with very considerable compression across the left side of the abdomen. The stomach, which was moderately full, had been compressed to such an extent as to empty it, vomit being thrown into the gullet. In this case death followed very quickly in my view, and I found no other material compression changes, intense asphyxia changes following the conditions described. In this case I found no external injuries of any material kind. Death was due to asphyxia from suffocation by compression due to crushing.

Q. So that, taking these as fair specimen cases, Dr, Simpson, and having heard the evidence of this mass of people here jammed together, would you agree that, the most probable cause of death, so far as it can be ascertained in the case of 173 people, would be asphyxia due to suffocation? A. Yes, sir.

Q. This, I take it, would be the result of people being pressed together in such a way that actually they could not employ the ordinary way of respiration? A. They could not move their chests and could not obtain oxygen.

Q. All breathing apparatus had been prevented from working - it really amounts to what has already been mentioned, asphyxia due to suffocation by compression? A. Yes.

Q. In some cases, I suppose, after a few moments of struggling, ensued a period of unconsciousness, and that period is much shorter than might be thought? A. In my opinion, from experience in other kinds of crushing by pinning and suffocation, unconsciousness may supervene within several seconds and death within fifteen and to twenty seconds.

Q. That is very often a maximum period? A. Certainly within a quarter to half a minute after respiration had ceased.

Q. The development of symptom of death is likely to be a quicker affair than is generally appreciated? A. Yes, if you once get factors which really do debar the inhalation of air, death may occur with great speed.

Q. The whole course of events would be over in less than half a minute; it is reasonable to suppose death did occur as speedily as that to a very large number of people? A. It is certain to me from my findings in these four cases, with the exception of the first one, in which case he remained alive for a short time. Circumstances there were different, and it was quite clear the pinning had not been in such a situation as could prevent him entirely from breathing.

*The coroner then addressed the jury saying:*

"You have heard the evidence of identification; you have heard the medical evidence; and you have had before you evidence which will show you how the actual death occurred. The remoter causes of the disaster I am not concerned with this morning and neither are you, and I am not going to comment on the various aspects of those causes because this court is not concerned. I am going to be very brief indeed.

"I am first going to draw your attention to the fact that the evidence before us is quite sufficient to dispel a number of the more sensational rumours which, no doubt, you have been acquainted with. There is nothing to suggest any stampede or panic or anything of the kind, and there is nothing to suggest that any particular section of the populace became victims of this disaster. Taking the names as a whole, they represent a cross-section of the populace of east London.

"Putting aside the more remote causes of the disaster, which are a very proper subject of the detailed inquiry, so far as we are concerned the fact is simple. Granted at this particular time the staircase was without centre rails; given the light which was so dim you couldn't see what was happening; and given the unfortunate fall of these people at the bottom it is only too plain and simple, I am afraid, what happened. In a moment, as you heard it described, there was a struggling mass of people. It was a dreadful thing to happen and I think you will also remember the account of the witnesses who were first called.

"They could hardly believe their eyes and it must have been shocking to hear a shout or a cry and, I imagine, two or three people had fallen down and then to see a mass of people struggling to free themselves, such was their position. It was a dreadful thing.

"There have been incidents of this kind before on a much smaller scale which shows how dangerous these establishments can be but this is a dreadful disaster and we can well imagine how the people who first saw the struggling mass of people hardly knew what to do next. They did try to effect rescues but found it impossible. Sufficient witnesses have told us it was almost impossible and it was only when police arrived in force that they again with great difficulty managed to free these poor people.

"And I want you to remember what Dr Keith Simpson said about the suddenness of death, because a good many people are inclined to think of a mass of people struggling, fighting and fainting. But that is not a true picture. There was a sudden mass fall as it were, and in a moment you had a vast heap of struggling people pinning each other down and in a very short space of time many of these died. That is the picture you must get in your minds, a sudden fall of people caught together and dying very quickly.

"Well now, as I say, this is not a case on which I propose to comment at all and the many matters which will have to be enquired into are not of immediate concern to us. Our duty is done and I want you, if you will, to just answer these three questions and return this slip to me."

After a short retirement the jury agreed they were satisfied that all the victims had been identified, and that death was from asphyxia from suffocation by compression, their verdict being that death was accidental. They also expressed their deepest sympathy for the relatives of the deceased.

The coroner: "That is a feeling shared by everyone in this court. We sympathise most fully with all those who have lost loved ones and friends in this terrible disaster."

# CHAPTER 6
## Blame and Responsibility

Members of the jury what you've heard so far has surely established in your minds a conviction that the councillors and officers of the borough of Bethnal Green were the victims of something close to collusion, however well-intentioned, by servants of the crown. There can be little doubt that officials learned at once, on the morning after the deaths on the staircase, that a tragic error had been made within the bureaucracy of the regional commissioners. This was demonstrated when the crowd control measures which the emergency committee had called for in 1941, and which were so lightly dismissed by the civil defence 'local expert', were implemented with such impressive celerity after the event.

The government promised a full inquiry, and then appointed as impartial inquisitor one of its own – I mean no disrespect here to Mr Dunne – to be managed by the ministry under investigation, home security. The findings of his tribunal, being found uncomfortably transparent, were then taken over, muffled and concealed ("we have therefore rearranged Mr Dunne's language" as Mr Morrison breezily remarked) in such a way that Bethnal Green council itself, after urgently and repeatedly warning of danger, came to be identified and vilified as the negligent culprit. And when the council tried to fight back by proposing to defend itself and say what it knew, it was threatened with the official secrets act.

Now you might argue, members of the jury, that all of that is very bad but what other course could the government have taken? At that point in the war, and with so many critical matters to address, ministers in important and high-profile positions could not afford to be suddenly exposed as dilatory or fumbling; they could not be weakened or diverted from the overriding goals. The affair had to be hushed up. A scandal would have damaged public morale.

But let us also remember what Mr Churchill had said in cabinet. "The government's position is unassailable." He spoke the truth; the alliance of Conservative, Labour and Liberal parties in both houses, the commons and the lords, was literally that. The prime minister stood high in public esteem; his cabinet stood together, working - so far as the public could see, at least - more or less harmoniously for victory. They knew, parliament knew, the country knew, there was no alternative. Individual elements might falter and fail but in the absence of a calamitous military defeat, the government could not.

Mr Morrison, who had said "the parliamentary responsibility is undoubtedly fully mine, and I accept it", could have taken another route. Instead of covertly propagating a nonsensical notion that the Bethnal Green accident had uncovered a dangerous psychological flaw in the behaviour of Londoners, the minister could simply and honourably have said that the safety measures appropriate to a shelter as big as Bethnal Green had been neglected, although he would prefer not to say how, that matters had been promptly rectified, but he should recognise that the system had, in this regard, failed and that in line with the honourable practice of ministerial responsibility he should stand down.

We can be sure that this, coupled with the existing draconian powers to guide and restrain the media would have silenced calls for the full dismal truth to be told, and Mr Morrison would surely have gained, among many if not all, admiration and respect. A man with his gifts of fluency and charisma, and his public standing, would have found his way back into office as the times changed. But resignation, as another public person was later to say in another context, was not among his virtues. He did not offer to quit and what was to follow makes matters, to us now sitting in judgment, a great deal worse.

Bethnal Green council quickly realised that the slaughter at the shelter would bring demands from the bereaved for compensation for the loss of parents, husbands, wives and children. But who should pay? Who should shoulder the burden of blame for what had happened?

# Metropolitan Borough of Bethnal Green

INDEXED

2 OCT 1941

BETH/36.

~~Enclosure.~~

A.R.P.
2-OCT 1941
RECEIVED

S. P. FERDINANDO
TOWN CLERK.

ALL COMMUNICATIONS
TO BE ADDRESSED TO
THE TOWN CLERK

EPHONE: ADVANCE 2410. 4831 Extn 279.

*Town Clerk's Office,*

*Town Hall,*

*Bethnal Green, E.2*

30th September, 1941.

Sir,

### Bethnal Green Tube Shelter - Surround at Entrance.

The General Emergency & Finance Committee at their meeting yesterday gave consideration to your letter of the 27th instant, stating that the Regional Commissioners were not prepared to approve the scheme for the provision of a surround at the entrance to the Bethnal Green Tube Shelter.

The Committee were of the opinion that the Commissioners could not have been in full possession of the facts in arriving at their decision, and I am desired by the Committee to emphasise the circumstances which prompted them to submit their proposal.

The iron railings of the Bethnal Green Gardens link up with two newly constructed brick pillars at each side of the entrance to the Shelter, and the structure between consists of a double wooden gate and a small wicket gate at the side.

The Committee are aware, in the light of past experience, that there is a grave possibility that on a sudden renewal of heavy enemy air attack there would be an extremely heavy flow of persons seeking safety in the Tube Shelter, and that the pressure of such a crowd of people would cause the wooden structure to collapse, and a large number would be precipitated down the staircase.

As the maximum number of persons which could comfortably be accommodated in the Shelter is 5,000, and it is estimated that in a heavy air raid approximately 10,000 people would seek shelter in the Tube, it will readily be gathered that a serious problem would evolve in the closing of the Shelter to the excess 4,000 unless some strong means of preventing their entry is provided.

It is not unusual for most of the larger shelters in the Borough to empty into the Tube Shelter during a heavy attack, and the Committee feel that there would be the possibility of a serious incident at the entrance to the Tube if the responsibility remained with the personnel alone to prevent the overcrowding of the Shelter.

In the light of this further evidence of the need for the erection of a strong gate to the entrance, I am directed by the Committee to request that further careful consideration shall be given to the matter, and that approval will be granted to the erection of the gate as suggested.

In the house of commons, Mr Morrison had said that "the local responsibility is primarily that of the local authority, in association with the regional commissioner". (As you doubtless notice, he did not add that the two bodies had differed over the need for special safety measures.) The word responsibility in the eyes and ears of ordinary people, looks and sounds like another word for "blame". Thus the council found itself identified as blameworthy, at least equally, with the civil defence authority. But of course the work of the civil defence administrators, even their whereabouts, was cloaked in secrecy to such an extent that even members of parliament complained that they could never contact its practitioners. The system was, for security reasons, more or less invisible and, to the public at large, not at all accountable.

Thus to the man in the street and until proved otherwise the blame and the guilt associated with the tragedy fell largely on Bethnal Green council, to become an abscess shrivelling and fading as the days and weeks passed, another wartime horror best forgotten - except for the person of Mrs Annie Amelia Baker of Braintree street, Bethnal Green.

She had been one of those who had struggled, shocked and dazed but alive, from the staircase on that March night. Her husband George, and her daughter Minnie, aged fourteen, did not survive. We have not heard their story nor are we likely to.

Sustained by funds raised by local activists, Mrs Baker took her case and her tale of bereavement to a firm of solicitors and issued a writ against the council alleging neglience in the running of the shelter and claiming damages for the loss of her loved ones.

At first and naturally enough Bethnal Green council assumed that if and when the case went to court the truth would come out and since the ministry and the regional commissioners knew the truth of the matter and also that, as local managers of the shelter, they were entirely under the authority of the ministry, those bodies would come to the rescue.

Stanley Ferdinando, the town clerk, sent a letter to that effect to the civil defence people inviting them to take on the burden of fighting the lawsuit. He wrote again, on May 19, 1943, pointing out that "following a visit to the shelter in October 1940, by the minister of home security with the [then] regional commissioner, admiral Sir Edward Evans, the Bethnal Green shelter was opened as it was on the same day and at his urgent request... the many communications and the whole course of action between the council and London civil defence region establishes that effective responsibility for construction, administration and safety of this shelter remained at all material times with the regional commissioners or the minister"

All ideas for improvements at the shelter had always been considered by the commissioners and their technical advisers, and whatever had to be spent was repaid by the treasury, Mr Ferdinando said. He also pointed out that the measures the council had earlier proposed "to prevent a crowd being precipitated down the staircase" had been dismissed by the regional technical adviser.

Mr Ferdinando (pictured, an image retrieved from the web) went on: "As litigation, present or future, will necessarily involve questions of national security about which the minister has publicly expressed anxiety, it appears to my committee that the defence to that litigation is eminently a matter which should be undertaken by London civil defence region or the minister, and further that the council should be relieved of all liability"

The town clerk mentioned that the borough's insurance policy covering such accidents had an upper limit of £5,000, which would not be enough to meet "the council's potential (and crushing) liability, should legal liability for damages be established against them, where 173 fatal and 61 non fatal cases have occurred".

Bethnal Green's letter was addressed to London civil defence. It did not reply but instead the town clerk received an icy blast from the ministry of home security, in the form of a letter signed by a senior official, Sir Oswald Allen.

"It was not clear to the minister", Sir Oswald wrote, "whether the council was contending that he or the regional commissioners were under a legal liability in respect of the deaths or injuries on the staircase". If they were, he said, "the minister would point out that the shelter was provided and maintained by the council in the discharge of its functions under the civil defence acts". Money spent on the shelter by the local council was reimbursed by the treasury after approval had been given, Sir Oswald acknowledged, and the minister had "a general responsibility to parliament for seeing that appropriate steps are taken for securing adequate protection to the public from aerial attack and the regional commissioners assist him in discharging the responsibility".

However, the minister believed, Allen said, that "none of these functions affects the legal position under which public shelter accommodation is provided and maintained by the local authority in its discharge of the functions entrusted to it by parliament. It therefore follows, in the minister's view, that any legal liability arising from the accident in question is wholly a matter for the council".

As Mrs Baker's claim was covered by the council's insurance, no question of the minister standing behind the council or making any contribution towards any damages if Mrs Baker won, appeared to arise. However, it was possible, Allen said, that if Mrs. Baker should succeed, claims by other persons might then follow. Because the council's insurance was limited to £5,000, the total cost would thus doubtless much exceed this figure.

"The question will then arise whether the minister will be prepared to make a contribution towards the expenditure of the council in dealing with those further claims or to ask the treasury solicitor to defend the council in any legal proceedings which may then ensue.

"The minister recognises that there are special circumstances in this case and at the appropriate time he will be prepared to give sympathetic consideration to the question of financial assistance".

The councillors and town clerk of Bethnal Green could now see that they were being hung out to dry. They could not have acted on their own initiative and at their own expense to make the shelter safer. If they had spent ratepayers' money without official approval on better crowd control, they'd have been in breach of their statutory duty and they risked being individually surcharged by the district auditor; they were legally required to get authority from civil defence and to be reimbursed by the treasury. But their requests for action had been rejected and now they were publicly blamed for the tragedy. If they tried to speak out they risked arrest and imprisonment for breaching the official secrets act. It was a travesty.

# CHAPTER 7
## A Glimpse of the Truth

More than a year elapsed before Mrs Baker's case came to court. The test action against the council appears to have ended on July 18, 1944, and was heard before Mr Justice Singleton in the King's Bench division of the high court. Members of the jury you would imagine that against such a sensational background, press and public would converge in large numbers on the courtroom, expecting that at last justice would prevail and the truth would be laid bare. It was not to be. The attorney-general, Sir Donald Somervell, was sent in at the behest of Mr Morrison, minister of home security, to apply for the case to be heard in camera, on the ground of national security.

Now you may ask yourselves, jurors, how could a piece of civil litigation in which an allegation of negligence by a local council was the central element, be a matter of national security to be judged in secret? Might there be a question of treason, or treachery? Or espionage, sabotage, betrayal? Nothing of the kind, just a civil dispute alleging negligence. This raised eyebrows among the lawyers and in due course led to a withering intervention by the then master of the rolls, Lord Greene. But of that, more in due course.

The hearing, in any event, went ahead with the doors locked and thus, in the absence of press coverage, there are no newspaper accounts of the day to day proceedings. All was not lost however; the journalists were kept out but Mr Justice Singleton was not to be thwarted from his day in the limelight. When the case concluded, media outlets were invited in, to be told that he had decided that the case was one of such importance that his judgment should be given in public. For what follows, I am grateful to the London Evening Standard, the Evening News and The Times variously on July 18 and 19, 1944.

"Judge says shelter steps were a trap" the Standard reported. In this, we can all concur - all that is except the minister of home security and the boss of London civil defence. But the conclusions and the reasoning which guided Mr Justice Singleton to his judgment will seem to us, in the light of what we know, more than somewhat questionable. He found for Mrs Baker and against Bethnal Green corporation, ruling that the council had been negligent in its management of the shelter.

Mr Justice Singleton announced his judgment by posing a rhetorical question: What was the cause of this most unfortunate accident? It seemed to him that the only inference to be drawn was that the block (the jam on the staircase) was caused by someone, or more than one, tripping or slipping on the unsafe steps, which took place before the firing of the guns, nor was there anything in the nature of rushing or surging.

Counsel for the defendants had put forward the explanation that the sole cause of the accident was the pressure on people on the staircase from those outside struggling to get in. Defence witnesses told the court that they had often visited the shelter and used the staircase and found no fault with it. But the judge brushed that aside saying "their attention had never been drawn to it" and that they had failed to notice the condition of the steps because the lighting was too poor. He discounted, or was perhaps unaware, of the effects of the blackout regulations.

The real cause of the tragedy, said Mr Justice Singleton, was the dangerous condition of the steps, combined with the very poor light, the lack of a handrail, the fact that there was no-one on duty on the steps or at the entrance and that those entering did not know that an accident had taken place and continued to hurry forward.

What was the state of knowledge, the judge asked, of those responsible for the management of the shelter? Evidence had been called for the plaintiff, Mrs Baker, as to accidents on the steps through people tripping, as to the defective light, and to the fact that those matters had been reported to the warden and assistant warden. They denied that any such reports or complaints had been made. He could not accept their denials, and was satisfied by the evidence of the plaintiff's witnesses that the condition of the steps and of the entrance had been brought to the notice of those responsible for managing the shelter.

With regard to the law, he was satisfied that Mrs Baker, her husband, and their daughter were licensees (had the status of persons permitted to use the shelter) and that the defendants had failed in their duty to them as such. The way down to the shelter was dangerous and unsafe and constituted a trap or concealed danger of which the defendants, through their agents, were aware.

In those circumstances the plaintiff was entitled to succeed in the action subject to the statutory defence raised under the personal injuries (emergency provisions) act, 1939, that the claim was barred on the ground that the matters complained of were "war injuries" in respect of which provision was made in the act. He was of the opinion, the judge said, that that defence failed. For several reasons he was sorry to arrive at that conclusion. He was told that the minister of pensions had treated the case as one of war injury and had granted a pension to the plaintiff. It might well be that Mrs Baker and her family would have been better off under the scheme as he knew that in such cases widows were treated generously by the government.

Mr Justice Singleton remarked that he could not leave the case without saying that it was only after a full consideration of all the evidence that he had arrived at his findings against the defendants. He had not overlooked the fact that many of those who gave evidence were voluntary workers, nor had he forgotten the difficulties of the times or the nature of the undertaking. Nonetheless the defendants had been in occupation of the shelter for two and a half years and nothing had been done to the unfinished steps.

He awarded Mrs Baker damages in respect of her husband on two counts, of £950 and £250, £250 in respect of her daughter, Minnie, and £100 in respect of her own personal injuries, making a total of £1550. In those times, this was a substantial sum, perhaps enough to buy a couple of modest houses in an average London district.

Jury, shall we agree that, in the light of what we know, even perhaps Mr Justice Singleton might agree, from what has gone before, that this outcome (apart from the largesse for Mrs Baker) was a woeful travesty of the judicial process, a product appropriate to the legend dreamed up in Whitehall. Bethnal Green council, if it had been set free from the steel claw of the official secrets act, could easily have argued that contrary to any supposed neglect it had been assiduous in trying to make safe the access to the shelter. But it was bound to silence by the terms lodged in Mr Morrison's white paper. Let us look again at that document's last paragraphs.

```
6. ... I have had a summary prepared for publication, modifying
the statements in regard to the psychological causes of the
disaster, but in no way modifying criticisms of errors of
commission or omission in administration. This summary has been
agreed by Mr. Dunne. It is embodied in the white paper...
7. The omission on security grounds of the main and proximate
cause of the disaster disturbs the balance of the report and
therefore prejudices those responsible for the administration of
the shelter in their defence against criticism induced by the
publication of Mr. Dunne's conclusions. I have tried to correct
this by sending a copy of the full text of the report to the
emergency committee of the local authority concerned for their
secret and confidential information. But their public defence of
their administration and any public statement which I make on the
subject must be restricted to matters which appear in the white
paper. H. M.
```

"therefore prejudices those responsible for the administration of the shelter in their defence against criticism of errors" ... who, reading those words could fail to conclude that the errors had been committed by the council, and that, "on security grounds" those "errors" could never be publicly examined? The fog of "national security" hung over the court and justice of any kind was vanquished. We shall go back to this matter but let us, before proceeding, demolish one of the learned judge's strictures, that the staircase itself was worn and dangerous. In fact the underground installations at Bethnal Green were only begun in the late 1930s and had only ever functioned as a deep shelter. Surviving photographs show us that the staircase was undoubtedly rough and ready but the ceaseless daily battering of commuters' boots and shoes had never existed here. The central line underground railway started to serve Bethnal Green and beyond only in 1946 and so it is unlikely that the concrete steps were unusually worn and dangerous.

Publication of the outcome of the trial brought the matter back into the public domain and Herbert Morrison's opponents now saw an opportunity to pile pressure on him. Several MPs, led by Sir Percy Harris, asked why it was considered necessary for the case to heard in secret.

"On the information before me at the time the proceedings began" Mr Morrison said "I felt bound to take the view that it would be contrary to the public interest that the case should be heard otherwise. For a similar reason, I do not feel able to indicate the specific grounds on which that decision was based". This seems to be a roundabout way of saying: "Because I felt like it" and it did not silence the critics.

Sir Percy expostulated: "This incident took place over eighteen months ago and the borough council have made it quite clear that there was no suggestion of panic? Does my right hon. friend not realise the bad impression that it makes to interfere with publicity in the courts, particularly in a neighbourhood where many people have suffered bereavement?"

The minister: "It would have involved the full discussion of a large amount of detail of what happens at either an air-raid incident or an incident connected with possible air-raid incidents. If that detail were published it would be information useful to the enemy. On balance, I came to the conclusion that it ought not to be published. The learned judge, however, gave his judgment in public, and, to that extent, the public has been informed. I noticed that my right hon. friend accused me in the press of hushing up the case. He knows me well enough to know that I would not hush up a case."

Commander Bower: "Isn't this only another example of that passion for secrecy without which we contrived to win the last war in less time than this one?"

Mr Morrison: "My hon. and gallant friend, not for the first time in his life, is quite wrong."

Mr Austin Hopkinson: "Can the right hon. gentleman give a definite assurance that the intention was not to protect the people mainly responsible?"

Mr Morrison: "I assure the hon. member that there was no wish whatever to protect anybody who might have been criticised if the affair had been public - not in the least. I think that this house knows me well enough to know that I do not protect people if they are guilty of inefficiency or of wrong conduct."

Mr Justice Singleton's interpretation of what had happened on the staircase was reviewed and modified later that year when Bethnal Green corporation asked the appeal court to overturn it. The hearing took place before three appeal court judges, the Master of the Rolls, Lord Greene, and two other judges, MacKinnon and du Parcq. In this case, counsel's source for this information is a law report published in the Times of December 9, 1944. An additional summary of both of these this judgmentscan also be found among the fragments – one might almost say, the wreckage – of Bethnal Green's own wartime archives at Stepney. (The file's designation is L/BGM/D/Z/18).

Lord Greene, the second most senior judge in the land, subjected the responsible minister (without actually naming him) to stinging criticism over the decision to have the hearing held in secret. In a written judgment, (part of which is inserted below, the blue pencil user's identity unknown) ) the master of the rolls endorsed the decision by Mr Justice Singleton to allow the government application but said it was unfortunate that instructions to the attorney general had been given. Nothing was more important than the public administration of justice and it would be "the greatest public misfortune if the idea should grow in the minds of the public or of government officials that the hearing of a case in camera would be ordered except for the most solid reason."

The master of the rolls said he was not suggesting that the ministry had acted otherwise than in what they thought to be the national interest. It was obvious that in time of war it was of the greatest importance that things which affected public security "in a real sense" should not be ventilated in public if there was even a possibility that to do so might help the enemy.

In such cases it would be right and proper that the very exceptional power of the court to hear cases in camera should be exercised. But in the present case, so far as he understood, the only ground of public security which influenced the mind of the ministry was the possibility that suggestions might come out in evidence during the case that there had been a panic.

In fact, he said "it was perfectly well known before the trial that there had been no panic". It was possible that some witnesses might, in evidence, describe the situation as one of panic but he could not regard a possibility of that kind as being a solid ground for departing from one of the cardinal rules for the administration of justice. Whether or not a witness said there had been a panic, the enemy would be quite astute enough to invent it.

Therefore "without casting any doubt on the good faith of the ministry" he felt constrained to say that an application for a hearing in camera should only be made for solid reasons. One of the dangers of making applications of that kind was that gradually, the conception of what was really necessary in the public interest became whittled down

until circumstances which should not be so regarded came, unconsciously and in good faith to be regarded as matters of public interest.

Mark this carefully, members of the jury, what comes next from Lord Greene: "The present case was one which led to a critical examination of what a public authority had done in performing its duty to the public and in which, conceivably, some officials of the ministry might have been subject to some kind of criticism" the judge said, cautioning that "those words must not be taken as a finding that such had been the case."

It had became apparent, the master of the rolls said, that although the ministry thought that the grounds on which they acted were solid grounds, "they were of the flimsiest description and should not have been allowed to outweigh the urgent public importance of maintaining the publicity of trials".

Members of the jury we are here entitled to surmise that Lord Greene was either demonstrating an extraordinary, almost psychic prescience of what had actually happened, or perhaps, in a quiet moment, some other legal luminary had murmured something in his ear that had informed and angered him. He did not actually speak the words "flimsy pretext" in reference to the actions of the ministry of home security but someone else was ready to do so, in the house of commons, and it came up early in 1945, from the MP for Wallasey, George Reakes. He and the two MPs for Bethnal Green, Sir Percy Harris and Dan Chater asked Mr Morrison to respond to the strictures from Lord Greene. "I hope to make a statement to-morrow" Mr Morrison replied.

The next day dawned but alas! Again, the hoped-for revelations were not forthcoming and nor was the minister. Instead, as MPs gathered expecting to learn at last how the tragedy and the mystery of Bethnal Green might now be fully explained, Mr Morrison did not appear and there rose in his stead, the chancellor of the exchequer, Sir John Anderson.

The house would remember, Sir John said, that the home secretary promised to come to the house and make a statement. Until a few minutes ago, he had fully intended to redeem that promise. "Unfortunately, however, he is suffering from a severe cold, and his doctor has just told him that it is imperative that he should remain indoors for at least 48 hours. Further, as the under-secretary of state for the home department is also not available, I have been asked to take the home secretary's place. I think it would be convenient to the house if I make it as a statement from him. I have here the statement and I [shall] make it as a statement from him without attempting the task of turning a direct form of speech into an indirect form."

Sir John then began to read, saying that Mr Morrison associated himself with everything the master of the rolls had said about the undesirability of cases being heard in camera. However, the judgment given by the master of the rolls showed that he was under the impression to quote the transcript - "the ministry knew perfectly well that there was no panic."

"At the material time I was relying for my information on the report made by Mr. Dunne of the inquiry which he held shortly after the disaster. As the names and addresses of the witnesses at the inquiry had been furnished to the solicitors to both parties to the high court action and it was reasonable to assume that the case would develop on similar lines, I do not think that the matter can now be seen in its proper perspective without disclosing Mr. Dunne's findings.

"Until recently security considerations have prevented the publication of his report, but after careful consideration I have come to the conclusion that circumstances have so changed that it can now be published. I have, therefore, arranged for publication of the report.

"The report divides the contributory causes of the accident into two categories - psychological and physical. The government decided in April, 1943, that public reference to the psychological cause might be an incitement to the enemy systematically to continue a form of attack which seemed likely to create a considerable disturbance to the life of the metropolis. There was the added possibility of heavy casualties being caused until structural alterations could be made to many underground shelters.

"I was however anxious to discharge as far as possible the undertaking I gave before Mr. Dunne began his investigations that the conclusions would, subject to security considerations, be published. Yet I was faced with the difficulty that the publication by themselves of the group of causes referred to by Mr. Dunne as physical causes, would disturb the balance of the report and have the effect of misleading any reader who had not had access to the full text.

"The conclusions recorded in the report appear to me to establish that the master of the rolls was under some misapprehension in making the remark I have quoted. In deciding whether application should be made for the hearing of the high court proceedings in camera, the position was that, so far from knowing that there was no panic, I had before me an opinion delivered by an experienced metropolitan magistrate, after a painstaking inquiry, that the effective cause of the disaster was that a number of people lost their self-control at a particularly unfortunate place and time.

"When the question of applying for the action to be heard in camera came before me, London had not long before been subject to renewed raiding, and in fact the case was heard when London was experiencing flying bomb attacks on a considerable scale. I therefore felt bound to take the view that it would be contrary to the national interest to run the risk of giving publicity by means of proceedings in open court to certain aspects of the inquiry and the general circumstances surrounding raids on London.

"First, undue attention would be directed to the less desirable but irremediable characteristics of design of some underground premises used as shelters which had served the public well.

"Second, the enemy could take note of the degree of alarm that raiding had been, and was even then, apt to inspire. Lastly on this information, the enemy might perhaps have been encouraged to make further efforts of the kind which, at that time at any rate, he appeared capable of making. In certain circumstances what happens on the ground and how the people take the raids may, I suggest, afford valuable information to those planning future attacks.

"The master of the rolls also expressed the view that the case was one in which conceivably some officials of the ministry itself might have been subjected to criticism, although he did not suggest that the possibility materialised.

"Mr. Dunne's report did in fact contain passages which animadverted on departmental administration and that of the local authority. My first intention was to publish those criticisms, omitting the passages which referred to the psychological causes of the disaster. But the whole balance of the report would thereby have been altered to the prejudice of all parties concerned and I was driven to deal with the report as a whole.

"In paragraphs 42–53 of the report, Mr. Dunne drew attention to the manner in which a proposal made by the borough council in August, 1941, for the replacement by a brick construction of the wooden hoardings surrounding the stairway had been dealt with at London regional headquarters. He did not suggest that the steps which might have been taken in connection with that proposal would have been adequate to prevent the accident, but I had his remarks brought at once to the notice of the officers concerned. [Counsel: That was demonstrably not true. The work was authorised by Sir Ernest Gowers on the afternoon of the day following the accident and began immediately.]

"The existence of these criticisms made me regret the necessity which I was satisfied existed for non-publication of the report, and while, as I have said, I do not wish to raise any controversy, I desire to assure the house that the decisions come to after serious consideration and on what seemed to me grounds of national security."

Members of the jury, see how smoothly the ministerial airbrush glides across the facts, blurring and fudging as it goes. What the council actually proposed – a six-foot baffle wall at the mouth of the shelter -

is crucial but the minister does not say that. What did it envisage? He does not say. How many times did the council raise the matter? "In August 1941" the Minister says; but the council raised the matter four times, in August, in September, in October, 1941, and then again in January 1942. Mr Morrison does not say they were four times refused, nor that they were told that a crush barrier and control of access would be a waste of money.

Was there really a panic? "I had before me an opinion by an experienced metropolitan magistrate" – but did Mr Dunne ever say (against the evidence) that there had been a panic, or was that part of the "changed language" that Mr Morrison mentioned to the cabinet? We hear once again, not that too many people were trying to pass quickly through a dangerous bottleneck, but that "the effective cause of the disaster was that a number of people lost their self-control at a particularly unfortunate place and time" - and we know that neither the enquiry nor the inquest threw up evidence to support that.

You will remember, members of the jury, that Mr Morrison did not appear in the chamber and that his words were delivered by another. This meant, of course, that the responsible minister was not able to deal with the questions that would naturally follow. From this distance it is perhaps uncharitable to wonder if there was any tinge of irony or sarcasm as Sir Percy Harris rose to say:

"May I first express my sincere sympathy with the home secretary and the under-secretary at the cause of their illness. The house will be anxious that they should soon recover. I should like to ask the right hon. gentleman if he realises that there are far more important issues than the personal attitude of the home secretary to a public inquiry. I should also like to know whether he is able to make any statement as to the position of the borough council in reference to the successful claim, both in the high court and in the court of appeal, for damages, and also the position of men serving overseas who are disbarred from making a claim because of the time factor?

Sir John replied: "I am in a little difficulty in dealing with any supplementary question, but I happen to know that the home secretary has been giving consideration to the matters which the right hon. baronet has just raised and that he had not felt that he was in a position to deal adequately with them, but I can assure the house that I will bring to my right hon. friend's notice what has just been said and

I am sure that he will, as soon as possible make a statement on those points."

Another MP, George Reakes, then launched his own flying bomb, saying to the absent home secretary that "I was more concerned with the remarks of the master of the rolls, particularly when he said that the [action by Mrs Baker against Bethnal Green] was held in camera on the flimsiest pretext. That is the reason why I tabled the question. It is not a question of the findings of the report. I had hoped the home secretary would have given something stronger than the mild reply which the right hon. gentleman has given us." Mr Reakes' missile produced no visible effect.

More questions came later in 1945 in the house but they were concerned mainly with the rights to compensation for East End servicemen who came home from the war to find that their loved ones had gone for ever. The days and weeks and months went by and as the chilly realities of postwar Britain became apparent, and peace was restored, any public appetite for any dwelling upon the horrors wartime London had endured withered away in the face of the tasks and the new perils that lay ahead.

Only in Whitehall did the Bethnal Green tragedy continue to occupy civil servants; this time though, not so much at the ministry of home security as the treasury. Mrs Baker's lawsuit served as a test action establishing the principle that the bereaved of the Bethnal Green disaster should be compensated. A secret compromise was reached whereby the borough did not attempt to take its appeal to the house of lords and accepted in exchange an agreement that its compensation bills would be met by the treasury. Thus it was that what might have been, back in 1941, a bill for £88 to put up a brick wall at the mouth of the staircase, turned into something very much more substantial. By December 31, 1950, six years after Mr Justice Singleton had found for Mrs Annie Baker, the amount paid out by the taxpayer via Bethnal Green corporation to various claimants, for the loss of life and trauma suffered, had risen to £69,554 8s 1d.

Not just that: home office file HO 205/201 discloses that when the accident was reviewed and analysed, engineers expected to spend some £7,000 on additional work to make safer the entrances to other deep shelters. Treasury approval to this effect was given at the end of March, 1943. A home office administrator wrote that "these safety measures followed the Bethnal Green incident and the work was carried out by contractors of the London passenger transport board." A year or so later and with work still going on, the cost had risen to £18,661 14s 5d. A total bill, then, for the bureaucratic oversight at Bethnal Green, not far short of £90,000, at 1940s prices. How many millions does that equal today?

Members of the jury you may feel it incredible that an episode such as this might remain concealed and forgotten for so long. And even now, we have not reached the end. Think back please to the evidence of the local civil defence official at Mr Dunne's enquiry, Mr William Joule Kerr. When, back in August 1941, he was asked to approve a less helter-skelter path into the staircase, one which would channel and slow down the flow of people, his concern seems to have been the expense, whereas his primary responsibility ought to have been the safe management of civilians in an extremely dangerous part of the capital. But perhaps Mr Kerr was not a resident of the east end, or it may be that he was overburdened with other pressing tasks. It is certainly possible. His superiors apparently did not know what his decision had been but, if they had, how would they have responded?

As we have seen, under questioning at the Dunne enquiry, Mr Kerr seemed to persist in denying that the pressure of crowds can become an unpredictable, irresistible force. A prudent official in such circumstances as Mr Kerr found himself, we may surmise, would have visited the staircase at a time when it was in heavy use and evaluated the dangers for himself. But he only went there in the daytime, with a borough engineer and did not, so far as can be seen, refer the matter to higher authority.

So what was the view of 'higher authority' – the judgment of Mr Kerr's boss, the head of London civil defence, Sir Ernest Gowers? Remember that Sir Ernest was a Whitehall mandarin, a distinguished political animal, not a civil engineer.

When the draft of the Dunne report was completed, a copy was sent to Sir Ernest for his observations. His response, perhaps, to our ears lacks any ring of contrition or regret, only a degree of condescension; it would be "unthinkable" that the inquiry findings should be published in full, he said, because of its propaganda value to the enemy. He misrepresents the fears expressed by the council and also criticises the investigator, saying that Mr Dunne "fumbles a bit; I fancy what he is trying to say is something like this:

"The local authority wanted to substitute a brick wall for the wooden barrier because they were afraid that when the shelter got full it might be impossible to close it effectively to further entrants; the crowd might break down the barrier.

"The regional technical adviser thought that the expense of a brick wall was not justified because the wooden barrier could be so strengthened as to remove this fear. When the accident happened the shelter was not in fact full, the barrier did not in fact break, and there is no reason to suppose that the regional technical adviser was wrong.

"But this cannot be regarded as disposing of the matter. The local authority had made formal representations to the regional commissioner that there was a grave possibility, in certain circumstances, that a large number of shelterers would be precipitated down the staircase.

"So serious an issue having been raised, the comparatively junior administrative officer ought not to have taken it upon himself to accept this grave responsibility on behalf of the commissioners; the question ought to have been referred higher; perhaps even up to the principal officer."

"I think there some substance to this criticism and I feel bound, as the person responsible, to accept it. But to say this is not to say that the decision was wrong, or that that it would necessarily have been different if taken at a higher level; on the contrary, I think that, if it had come to me, I should probably have upheld the decision, knowing that this risk is inherent in all deep shelters approached by stairs and that this particular shelter had been safely used by thousands of people night after night during the worst of the London bombings". This statement comes from the same man who, sixteen or so hours after the tragedy had briskly authorised an elaborate and comprehensive transformation of the entrance to the shelter.

One is bound here to suspect that Sir Ernest is either wilfully misunderstanding the issue or is offering an analysis not entirely dispassionate, rather he seems to be taking up a defensive position for London civil defence based on the 'never apologise, never explain' theory of Whitehall bluster.

Set that against this summary of how the councillors of Bethnal Green bore the brunt of undeserved public anger for the disaster. It occurs in a letter written to the ministry of home security on January

2, 1945, by the council's solicitor, William Easton.

Mr Easton announced that Bethnal Green corporation had decided not to appeal to the house of lords in the case of Mrs Baker's claim, because of an agreement between the minister of home security and the council to the effect that "no step in the defence should be taken without the approval of the treasury solicitor and he did not support an appeal".

Mr Easton went on: "We understand that it is desired that we are now to proceed to negotiate a settlement of all claims of which notice has been given, though in some cases they may be statute-barred. Nothing, however, is to be offered without first obtaining your, or the treasury solicitor's approval to any settlement. Our negotiations are for the moment to be of an exploratory nature.

"We should like to add that our clients have felt very deeply the reflections which have been passed on them by the court of appeal and by the judge in the court below. They have had to bear the whole brunt of the attack.

"You may recall that (in 1940, shortly after it was opened) our clients had closed this shelter but that they were directed to re-open it. That long before this disaster happened they were informed that the maintenance of the shelter was in the hands of the ministry and that whilst the court of appeal rejected the finding of the judge that the cause of the accident was defective steps, they held that it was brought about by lack of control and bad lighting.

"The ministry had informed the council that it had been arranged with the commissioner of police that in air raids the entrance to the shelter would be controlled by the police which in fact was not done on this occasion and, as to the lighting, this was in accordance with the regulations then in force.

"All our clients had, beside the chief and deputy warden, were six wardens, that again in accordance with official directions, who in no circumstances could possibly control a crowd such as endeavoured to enter the shelter that night. Our clients have all along felt that had they been judged by the Dunne report they would have escaped the opprobrium passed on them.

"The hearing before the trial judge was extremely unsatisfactory to say the least, a few witnesses out of about sixty called at the inquiry were selected to give evidence for the plaintiff. The defendants could not call the many others who gave evidence at the inquiry, as since the latter they had been induced to join an association to prosecute their claims and most of them were plaintiffs in other actions and their views in consequence had naturally undergone a change adverse to the council.

"Our clients have received a sum of £5,000 from their insurers in full satisfaction of their liability under the policy, but this sum will be exhausted in the costs of the defence, the disbursements made and to be made in this connection amount to £3,,660"

It has not been possible to trace what reply the ministry made to Mr Easton but three days later, one of its officials, Mr Arthur Edmunds sent a copy of the letter to officials at London civil defence remarking that some of the statements were "disingenuous" but that "their validity cannot fail to have a bearing on the awkward question we now have to consider, viz., the extent to which the council are to be given exchequer assistance in meeting the financial burden resulting from the legal proceedings.

"We should be glad if you would be good enough to have all the relevant regional records examined, and let us have your comments in the light of what they reveal.

"As regards the statement that the council had closed the shelter but were directed to reopen it, my recollection is that in the course of an exploration of the region's Bethnal Green file at a much earlier stage I came across a copy of a minute by the minister, dated early in October, 1940, ordering the shelter to be opened. I never succeeded in finding the original of the minute or tracing the file (if indeed there was one) on which it was written."

Mr Edmunds suggested contacting other officials now posted elsewhere who might help but admitted that parts might be missing from the regional records – "and I fully anticipate that you will".

"The solicitors support by reference to specific documents" Mr Edmunds continued " the statements that the council were informed before the disaster (a) that the maintenance of the shelter was in the hands of the ministry and (b) during raids the entrance to the shelter would be controlled by the police. No doubt you will be able to trace the documents which the solicitors mention. As regards the point they make about the wardens, it may be true that the council were given instructions about the number of wardens to be employed in shelters as a whole but I cannot imagine that directions were issued by the region as to the strength of the service in individual shelters."

This stout defence of Whitehall's actions was copied to Sir Ernest Gowers who, of course, was no stranger to the ways of Whitehall. It made him uneasy.

"I do not like the look of this at all" he wrote. "We seem to have based our answer to the town council's letter on an instinctive repudiation of liability rather than on an examination of the facts of the case. It does not seem to me to be right for a government department, however natural in a private individual in such circumstances. The town council's second letter seems to me to have much point." Just how that went down at the ministry we do not know.

# CHAPTER 8
## The Civil Defenders

Members of the jury, you could be forgiven for feeling somewhat fatigued at this relentless bombardment. As this story has unfolded, you may perhaps have wondered why counsel should have sought to put such a matter before you. What could, or should be done? A verdict may be reached but nothing can be changed; it was almost a lifetime ago and in the broad context of the second world war, a secondary episode. (Although not, of course, to those still surviving, who suffered bereavement.) There was so much destruction and futile slaughter, a catalogue of horror across Europe and Asia, on land, in the air and at sea. As Churchill remarked to the cabinet when Morrison mooted a public inquiry into the calamity: "I am against giving such limelight to this incident. What notice is taken of all who died in air attacks?"

The difference, jury, is that the world now knows plenty about those great and terrible events; the Bethnal Green affair was a home-made blunder, a piece of neglect that even to this day is obscured and disregarded. The bombings, atrocities, genocide, were conscious acts of malignant ideology, malevolence for which, some at least, were punished. Here was lethal muddle and bungling by our own people. It didn't have to happen and, when it did, was quickly swept out of sight on that ground so freely and usefully invoked nowadays – "national security". Something like it could even happen again; think perhaps of this when you make your way down a crowded public staircase, jostling in a city teeming with hurrying people. Think of the Lawsons shepherding little Tony and the toddler Patricia, just two years old, from their home in Roman Road to the hoped-for safety of the Bethnal Green shelter and, even there, meeting a horrible, needless death. They should have been safe and were not. Think too of the shattering effect on the people who had managed the shelter and staffed it - councillors, wardens and staff of Bethnal Green, who had seen the danger, tried to warn and now, though blameless, faced contempt and obloquy. They were not even allowed to defend themselves. As one relative has told counsel: "I was always told the true story, and was aware of the huge impact the cover-up had on the family. Because of the fall-out from that official spin, my grandparents gave up their life in London and moved north". Percy Bridger, the former mayor and husband of Mrs Margaret Bridger, then the current mayor of Bethnal Green, who had until then dedicated his life to public service, never entered public life again. He is said to have suffered a nervous breakdown because of the things he saw in the shelter that night, no doubt compounded by the vitriol directed at him locally.

That is why, members of the jury, we should give at least a little of our time to this. We have seen some of the testimony given before Mr Dunne; a fairly small amount of the whole and even that has been compressed. But counsel has sought at all times to be fair and balanced and, unlike Mr Morrison, we have not changed the language. But before we embark upon the business of detecting and allocating responsibility, let us acquaint ourselves with the status of the crown and its myriad offshoots in the matter of civil defence and wartime shelter policy. For this we can thank Mr Macdonald Ross who, as Mr Dunne began the task of compiling his findings, sent him this history of the origins of current civil defence policy. For ease of comprehension it too has been somewhat telescoped. This note preceded the document itself:

```
Mr Dunne - This is a rather hurried effort,
but I think it covers all of the points
that affect the inquiry.
Ian Macdonald Ross. 19/3
```

```
(1) The conception of Regional Commissioners as agents of the
government under emergency conditions first took shape in 1938.
The idea which persisted right until the outbreak of war was that,
from the inception of hostilities there would be intensive
bombing on a scale which would not merely disrupt communications
but would absolutely isolate and insulate sectors of the country.
```

It was intended, therefore, that the regional commissioners, in the event of this drastic severance of communications, should have, within the limits of their respective regions, the full powers of a regular government. To all intents and purposes, they would act as they thought best in the public interest, and on the restoration of communications they would be indemnified by the government ex post facto for any acts which conferred a liability of any sort.

(2) In point of fact, the course of events was quite different... there was no appreciable bombing for a year and when aerial warfare got into its stride, the ruptures of communications were temporary and local. It was therefore necessary to adapt to the actual trend of events and the result has been that the regional commissioners' status is very confused and complicated.

(3) The commissioners were appointed by royal warrant and there is therefore no act creating or specifying their functions. They are not mentioned in either the A.R.P. act 1937 or the civil defence act, 1939. Their functions, to the best of my knowledge, fall into three main classes, statutory functions under the defence regulations, functions delegated administratively by the minister of home security and other government departments, and functions specifically conferred by royal warrant. These delegations cover a very wide field including a good deal of air raid shelter work. The functions conferred by the warrant are those of coordinating and controlling all measures of civil defence. The theory has been that control, as distinct from coordination, should operate only when the region is isolated but this distinction has been to some extent obscured by the wide powers exercised by the commissioners either as agents of the minister (wielding the sharp instrument of exchequer grant) or as designated delegates under the defence regulations.

(4) For the purpose of the inquiry it would seem sufficient to consider the respective spheres of the commissioner and of the local authority

(i) in relation to air raid shelter administration generally, and

(ii) in relation to the particular proposals submitted to London region by Bethnal Green council regarding the entrance to the tube shelter.

(5) The primary responsibility for the provision of air raid shelter rests with the local authority. Even this is less simple than is commonly supposed but is none the less real and inescapable. Before the war broke out it was contemplated that

all local authorities would prepare and submit to the A.R.P. Department of the home office (now the ministry of home security) schemes of air raid precautions. These schemes were to include, and did include, proposals for the provision of public shelter. There were then, of course, no regions and the schemes were dealt with centrally by the home office. The main points which would be considered would be

(i) the scale of protection in relation to the size and assumed vulnerability of the district, and

(ii) the general type of shelter proposed. These schemes were very rudimentary and in the event none was ever formally approved. The Munich crisis fell into this period and produced a great deal of slit trench provision.

(6) General statements of government shelter policy were made in December 1938 and April 1939, but the details were not worked out and circulated to local authorities until April 1939. These details .. set out in 1939 .. included the appointment of regional technical advisers directly responsible to the chief engineer of the home office. Their primary duty was to "advise and assist local authorities in carrying out shelter policy."

(7) There was now a great drive to produce additional forms of shelter rapidly and the practice was introduced of publishing stereotyped designs and of allowing local authorities to carry out the work with the approval of the technical advisers .. [they] were given further powers in March 1940 but there was no change of principle, except that, by this time the regional commissioners had been appointed and the technical advisers were attached to regional headquarters. (Their relationship to the commissioner was advisory only; constitutionally they were responsible to an official called the 'regional officer' who was both an adviser of the commissioner and an outpost of the ministry of home security.

(8) The main change came in June, 1940, when the minister of home security delegated to regional commissioners the powers conferred on him by paragraph 3 of defence regulation 29A. These powers enabled regional commissioners to issue to local authorities such instructions, either general or detailed, as to the provision of air raid shelters, as they might consider necessary in the light of local circumstances. The circular emphasised that the assumption and delegation of the powers of direction in no way abrogated the responsibilities with which local authorities are charged for securing the provision or adequate shelter.

(9) Since June, 1940, therefore, the regional commissioner

has had three main sources of authority (and responsibility) in relation to shelters, viz:-

(i) As administratively designated agent of the ministry, he has had the general control of the finance of air raid shelter work, that is to say, the grant (now 100%) is, with few exceptions, administered regionally (subject to general over-riding directions given by the ministry). This, I should say, is in practice his strongest weapon.

(ii) Partly in virtue of the powers delegated under defence regulation 29a and partly as agent of the ministry, he has administrative responsibility for ensuring that the shelter constructed locally conforms to the current standards and specifications issued from time to time by the chief engineer and is provided on a scale adequate to meet the needs of the area.

(iii) Partly in virtue of powers delegated … and partly as administrative agent of the ministry of home security and ministry of health, the regional commissioner has a general responsibility for the supervision of air raid shelter provision and also of the actual user of shelters.

(10) Apart, therefore, from the question of finance, the commissioner's responsibility for air raid shelter work is, and must be, exercised on general lines; the responsibility for detail, and in all cases the initial responsibility, rests with the local authority. The only exception to this principle would seem to be where a specific individual case is submitted by the local authority to the region; here, I think, there is no escape from the fact that the region's responsibility is increased. To what extent it is increased would seem to depend on the particular circumstances of any given case. If, for example, a local authority contends that the strutting of a particular basement is inadequate and should be improved, and if the region take the opposite view, then the region must I think assume responsibility for leaving the shelter as it is.

(11) The dividing line - the relative degree of responsibility - is particularly difficult to assess where, as in the Bethnal Green case, neither the local authority nor the region foresee the real nature of the potential danger which has to be safeguarded against. They did not really foresee the danger and I question whether in the circumstances obtaining at the material date anybody else dealing with would have foreseen it. On the whole, however, I should have thought that the local authority with their detailed local knowledge, their great experience of the actual users of the tube, and their opportunities for a practical examination of all the difficulties likely to arise at

this very exceptional shelter, must be quite definitely held to be primarily responsible: I think the region have a substantial responsibility but I also think the interest and responsibility of the local authority preponderates. It is impossible to represent these things numerically, but if an attempt had to be made I should not put the [technical adviser's] interest higher than 2/5. It may not have been so much as that, for the shelter is probably unique in several ways and nobody but the local authority with their first-hand knowledge of local conditions could have foreseen the possible effect of this uniqueness.

(12) Finally, it is important to remember in partial absolution of both the local authority and the regional technical adviser, that the problem is not confined to this shelter though probably it is presented there in a particularly acute form. It is asking a good deal to expect a junior regional official and the deputy surveyor of a smallish borough to predict conditions, the possibility of which would depend to a considerable extent on a modification of the enemy's raiding tactics. It is true that the local authority give the appearance of having predicted something rather similar to what happened and to that extent they are rather hoist with their own petard.

Ian Macdonald Ross 18/3/43.


Jury, this document starts in a factual and judicious way but as it goes on it veers and swoops into something of a polemic; please read again that last sentence of paragraph 12. "It is true that the local authority give the appearance of having predicted something rather similar to what happened and to that extent they are rather hoist with their own petard" (this archaic metaphor implying that some kind of explosive device has gone off in the hands of a person intending to use it against another). If, as Mr Macdonald Ross seems here to acknowledge, the local authority was best placed to judge, its recommendations on safety should have prevailed. But they did not. And he also appears to be suggesting that, because Bethnal Green council foresaw the calamity, or something like it, it was their fault that it was not averted. Can there be any other interpretation? But in the preceding paragraph, he had written: "...neither the local authority nor the Region foresee the real nature of the potential danger which has to be safeguarded against. They did not really foresee the danger ... "

This reasoning seems, jury members, perverse and convoluted. It is inescapable that the council recorded its fear that something very bad might happen on the staircase and unarguable that it repeatedly communicated that concern. It had inherited, for the duration of the war, an underground shelter which the government required it to manage for its community as an effective albeit rudimentary refuge from devastating enemy attack; it readily undertook this important work but it did not have, and could not be expected to have, any specialist knowledge of things that might go wrong. That, if words are allowed to have their proper meaning, was the business of the supposed experts of the ministry of home security. The borough had warned the controlling authority time and again, that the potential hazard ought to be dealt with; and in paragraph six of Mr Macdonald Ross's memorandum, it is implied that Mr Kerr could and should have consulted the chief engineer at the ministry of home security in cases where uncertainty existed. But he did not and the council's appeals were loftily dismissed. What is the point of making recommendations if they are repeatedly ignored? The danger was foreseen as, in the cabinet discussion in April 1943, the Chancellor, Sir Kingsley Wood, had remarked. The warnings were ignored and that is the central fact that the servants of the crown strove to conceal.

The crown's wartime shelter policy, in spite of the legalistic gloss imparted here by Mr Macdonald Ross, was the product of ad hoc improvisation made at the gallop. How could it have been otherwise? The policy of the pre-war governments, of Stanley Baldwin and Neville Chamberlain, had been to try to bluff against Hitler and hope for the best. We know how that turned out. It follows that in 1939 nobody knew what to expect and no government wanted to spend against what might not happen unless and until it was presented with an overwhelming case.

# CHAPTER 9
# The Guilty Men?

So, men and women of the jury, you will surely agree that what has gone before in this investigation provides strong evidence of culpable negligence, of concealment of that negligence and of attempts to thwart and pervert the natural processes of establishing the truth.

Shall we then discuss who might we convict, and of what? The death of one-hundred-and-seventy-three people came about neither by act of God nor by collective suicide. The victims were overwhelmingly civilian caught in a war which their own government had declared against a foreign aggressor; the crown acknowledged that it had a duty to protect its citizens so far as it was able and it caused the local authority to take charge of an available local installation to that end. It provided funds and purported to supervise the administration of the shelter; but then its servants ignored a sensible and well-founded recommendation to make safe the entrance to the staircase. When it was confronted with the facts of the disaster it moved swiftly to adapt and improve upon what had earlier been proposed. A reasonable person would say that action spoke louder than any words.

In this case members of the jury let us, at least briefly, consider an extreme verdict: that here was a case of involuntary manslaughter - the unlawful killing of human beings without malice aforethought but by criminal negligence. There was no intention to kill, only culpable neglect of duty; negligence in the provision of reasonable safety. The council had repeatedly warned, as we have seen, that in the event of heavy sudden pressure, the staircase could be a death trap and it suggested measures to restrain and slow down the anxious crowd that used it. It drew up a modest plan of works and asked for sanction to make it happen. That proposal was not given a chance to succeed; it was not referred to any competent civil engineering specialist for evaluation but was dismissed out of hand because it would cost the sum of £88. "A waste of money" was Mr Kerr's exact, succinct phrase.

Counsel has outlined to you this possibility of bringing such a charge against those who had the power to act but did not do so, namely the ministry of home security and the regional commissioner. But reflecting upon the matter one sees that too much time has elapsed for such a conviction to be obtained. Those documents which survive suggest culpable negligence by individuals, but defence counsel could persuasively argue that there was too much uncertainty; it may be that the civil defence official who is on record as dismissing the proposal actually favoured it but was informally advised against it by a superior; or that his decision was taken in the context of extreme pressure to cut costs from elsewhere; or that the prevailing wisdom was that a resumption of enemy bombing on a large scale was unlikely.

Only by questioning knowledgeable officials could we determine how the process stood and, at this time of writing nearly seventy years later, that is not possible. For a charge of involuntary manslaughter by criminal negligence to succeed, a jury would want to see a much stronger body of documentary evidence than can be brought to bear by scrutiny of those documents that remain. Counsel should add, of course, that this possibility of a formal charge of negligence has not been uniquely conjured up by the prosecution; consider this little message from the minister himself to Sir Ernest Gowers at civil defence headquarters on March 5, 1943, just as work began belatedly to reconfigure the entrance after the tragedy. Mr Morrison says, among other things: "I note the steps that are being taken in regard to the Bethnal Green shelter itself. It may be that the latter will be interpreted in some quarters as an admission of neglect but if they are judged necessary they ought not to be delayed on that account." This may seem very mild terminology but set against the customarily affable or at least neutral language of Whitehall it will have carried an unpleasant sting.

Shall we then, men and women of the jury, try to list those holders of office under the crown who might be deemed responsible, in some degree or other, for what happened, or to blame for the suppression of the truth? The prime minister, Winston Churchill? Herbert Morrison? The home office and its half-sister the ministry of home security? Laurence Dunne? The metropolitan police? William Kerr and his boss Sir Ernest Gowers? The metropolitan borough of Bethnal Green, now long defunct and subsumed into the London borough of Tower Hamlets?

All might be admitted, in one way or another, to be part-culpable. But in the public domain, at the time this work was assembled, the record shows that blame attaches officially only to Bethnal Green. It was judged and convicted in the court of King's Bench of negligence and the verdict, adjusted by the court of appeal, still stands. Compensation to survivors and relatives of the victims was paid by the borough of Bethnal Green, quietly reimbursed by the treasury. At least the taxpayer forked out for this piece of incompetence, rather than the impoverished and much-bombed residents of Bethnal Green. As the solicitor, William Easton wrote: "They have had to bear the brunt of the attack". As she proceeded through the streets near her home, the mayor of Bethnal Green, Mrs Margaret Bridger, endured jeers of "you cow"; and other councillors were openly called "murderers". Nobody could explain that they were innocent of supposed negligence at the shelter, that they had warned of the danger on the staircase and had been rebuffed; the threat of prosecution under the official secrets act, saw to that.

In the view of counsel, if there was any culpability on the part of the councillors and officials of the Bethnal Green Council, it amounted only to an excess of deference to officialdom, an assumption that loyal and silent acquiescence in wartime in all matters was of supreme value; and a degree of incoherence and hesitation in their exposition of the perceived danger.

We cannot know what Bethnal Green's councillors and officials said to each other because (so far as counsel can establish) all such records have disappeared. We need not pretend that the council and those who served it were excessively noble and virtuous; Mr Dunne's enquiry turned up trifling accusations against the shelter wardens, of laziness, arrogance and self-interest. Maybe some were true; some were surely malicious. But broadly speaking, members of the jury, you should acquit the council.

What about Churchill? He was certainly the boss and understood the implications of the case. The home office delivered to him a special secret briefing on the matter. Indeed, most of the source material that has been laid before you is derived from home office or ministry of home security files; and yet counsel first became aware of the lurking truth behind the Bethnal Green tragedy from extracts in a little bound volume of transcribed copies, prepared for the prime minister's office, a volume designated PREM 4/40/15 which may be found at the national archives. Copies of relevant documents in the case are there, neatly bound in a blue rexine-covered A4 book, which covers the period only from 1941 to 1943. There is a copy of Mr Ferdinando's letter of September 30, 1941 (but not the council's other letters), there too are copies of Mr Kerr's correspondence with the council and his own bosses about his decisions. (Incidentally, jury, if you look through these papers, you will find absolutely nothing that pertains either to the psychology of the local people nor to the notion of Luftwaffe bomber pilots casting around for London shelter targets where hysteria might be generated.) Why would such a file have been prepared for the prime minister? Only, surely, to enable him to evaluate the weight of potential damage to the administration if the matter leaked out.

We can be sure that the political implications were not lost upon the prime minister: he would know at once that here was the nucleus of an almighty row, a scandal that could bring questions in the house, a bad press around the world and ministerial resignations. As a war leader under continuous, frightful pressure, Mr Churchill surely could have spared little time or thought for this mess; he may have reasoned that he could afford to lose the responsible minister, Morrison, but he could not afford wobbles in the cabinet, gloating voices from the enemy in Berlin, and a fiercely critical glare lighting up the shadowy work of London civil defence. Jury, few of us could imagine the calculations, the tensions and the pressures upon him at that stage of the war; in a pugnacious phrase (as we have seen) he rallied the cabinet to reassure them: "we are unassailable." By saying, he made it so, and Mr Morrison and Mr Macdonald Ross and Mr Dunne went to work. Broadly, we must exonerate Mr Churchill. He was a warrior prince with victory at any cost his only perspective. He existed at a level that even now we can barely glimpse.

The police perhaps? If officers had been posted at the entrance, their restraining presence might have slowed the hurrying crowds. But they were too thinly spread. Mr Dunne discussed the question in his report and concluded

"it was certainly unfortunate that on this particular night there was no constable at the shelter for some ten minutes after the alert ... as to whether he could have done anything, and what, it is idle to speculate; I am satisfied that police were despatched to the shelter as rapidly as they became available. Within a few minutes there were a sergeant and ten constables on the spot and this contingent was further and rapidly increased. By 8.45 an inspector, a sergeant and 15 constables had arrived and thereafter rescue work was organized rapidly and effectively. By about 9.15 there were a chief inspector, two sub-divisional inspectors, an inspector and some sixty constables ... the opinion I have formed is that the superintendent and his senior subordinates are zealous, experienced and efficient officers, who have organized the policing of the division along lines which experience had hitherto shown would best combine efficiency with the necessary economy in manpower."

We can agree, members of the jury, that officers could have been assigned to the shelter and their presence would almost certainly have made a difference; and it was generally foreseen that a heavy reprisal raid might be launched against London at this time; but so far as we have seen, no mechanism existed for the police to take account of potentially hazardous behaviour by anxious crowds. They already had plenty to do and could not know in advance where they might be needed.

You will notice that counsel included the investigator, Mr Laurence Rivers Dunne, among those who might be deemed culpable in this matter, at least so far as to assisting in the cover-up. Let us look a little more closely.

Mr Dunne was very much a creature of what used to be called the establishment; Eton, Magdalen College, Oxford, infantry service in the first world war, rising to the rank of major; an excellent shot; three times mentioned in despatches, from Flanders, Salonika and Trans-Caucasia. When the 1914-18 war was over, he went into the law as a barrister, metropolitan magistrate, at Marylebone in the thirties and then Bow Street. He married and had a son (killed in 1944) and a daughter (who also predeceased him). He held what would have been called 'traditionalist' views in those times but would now be described generally as reactionary; he was an admirer and a disciple of Lord Goddard, (soon to become the lord chief justice) and like him favoured such penalties as hanging, flogging and lengthy jail terms. He became recorder of east Berkshire and later chief metropolitan magistrate, was knighted in 1948 and died, aged 76, in 1970.

The transcript of the Bethnal Green inquiry is a better memorial to Mr Dunne than his official report. It shows that his questioning of the survivors and the bereaved was kindly and broadly sensitive; his examination of witnesses generally was incisive and purposeful, but tolerant. We do not know what he thought of his ministerial minder, if that is what Mr Macdonald Ross was, because the only messages that come to light between them are not from him. There is a letter from Mr Dunne to the home secretary, responding to amiable words of thanks from the minister; Mr Dunne expresses great appreciation for having had the opportunity to serve, etc. It says nothing much.

The mystery that lingers over Mr Dunne and his report, members of the jury, concerns two of the characters that we have heard from at some length - the head of London civil defence, Sir Ernest Gowers, and the town clerk of Bethnal Green, Mr Stanley Ferdinando. We have seen that Sir Ernest was invited to comment upon Mr Dunne's report and did so ("I fancy what he is trying to say .. etc") but only in a breezy reply to the home office.

His name does not appear on the list of people called to testify before Mr Dunne. And yet he was the high official with ultimate responsibility for shelter safety in London where, in the same month, a terrible tragedy had befallen shelterers. Was there no question that Mr Dunne might want to put to him? Was there no defence, or justification, or explanation, that he might want to put forward for inclusion in the report? And Mr Ferdinando, a trained lawyer who, in his capacity as clerk to the borough council had repeatedly sought to draw attention to the perceived hazard on the staircase. Might he not have been questioned? "What happened to make the councillors want to raise this matter, Mr Ferdinando?" Or "you did not really foresee this tragedy, did you?" - two possible questions that come to mind. But Mr Dunne did not ask them to tell their stories, or maybe was dissuaded from doing so, members of the jury, and you should ask yourself why that is. An inquiry that did not trouble to question these two central characters is either a very casual affair or one that assumes that some testimony is better left unrecorded.

After all, the home secretary, Mr Morrison, had announced the inquiry in the commons on March 10, saying that "without in any way assuming that there was negligence in any quarter, the government wish to be assured, and wish the public to be assured, that any avoidable defect either in the structure and equipment of the shelter, or in the arrangements for its staffing, or for the supervision of those within the shelter, is brought to light." Few could have shed more light than these two men. But it seems as if Mr Dunne yielded to pressure to follow an alternative agenda; in his questioning of witnesses, the investigator returns, again and again, to the theme of panic at the mouth of the shelter; of a crowd supposedly driven to madness by fear of an approaching bomber fleet and the shattering roar of rocket batteries. It would have been a proper line of questioning even if it had not been urged upon him by Mr Macdonald Ross. But with a few mild exceptions, the answer came back: No, we tried to get in but we were stuck in an immovable jam. It was too dark to see anything.

And yet, in the report that bears his name, there is inscribed:

"May I conclude with two short propositions?

(a) This disaster was caused by a number of people losing their self control at a particularly unfortunate place and time.

(b) No forethought in the matter of structural design or practicable police supervision can be any real safeguard against the effects of a loss of self control by a crowd. The surest protection must always be that self control and practical common sense, the display of which has hitherto prevented the people of this country being the victims of countless similar disasters."

You may feel it hard to believe that one who had sat through several days of evidence about the tragedy could volunteer such an analysis. No forethought in the matter of structural design? Shortly before these words were being written, the extensive rebuilding of the entrance to the staircase had been officially approved as a top priority by the chief engineer and the head of London civil defence.

A number of people losing their self-control? The testimony produced little or no evidence of that and some decisive refutations; and in any case most of the victims were girls and boys and older women. The word "panic" appears principally in the briefing document urged upon Mr Dunne by Mr Ian Macdonald Ross. Look again at what the Shoreditch coroner, Mr W R H Heddy, said to the inquest jury: "...the evidence before us is quite sufficient to dispel a number of the more sensational rumours which, no doubt, you have been acquainted with. There is nothing to suggest any stampede or panic or anything of the kind..."

Or consider this question sent to all civil defence technical officers, just after the disaster, by the home office chief engineer: "Are there means of controlling entry of a crowd so that there is not undue pressure at the bottleneck or at the head of staircases and steep slopes?"

Surely we must conclude that this is the crux in Mr Dunne's report where Mr Morrison's remark "We have therefore altered Mr Dunne's language" is to be applied. The story of how the council tried to make the staircase safer appears in the report, but in a distant, muffled form; it is represented as something generally irrelevant and the refusal of the civil defence people to agree is not mentioned. It was glossed over and it was again glossed over when Mr Morrison made his commons statement in the closing weeks of the war. It was not allowed to surface when Mr Justice Singleton sat in judgment in the action against Bethnal Green corporation by Mrs Annie Amelia Baker.

Mr Dunne did not know what we know now – what the cabinet had said and done about keeping the tragedy out of the public eye – but he certainly knew more than most. Instead he kept loyally silent; loyal, that is, to the minister and the crown. But, members of the jury, bear also this in mind – that it is conceivable he did not remain totally silent; the sceptical might wonder how it was that the master of the rolls, Lord Greene, could be so confidently scathing in his criticism of the authorities over the matter of getting the Baker case to be held in camera. Mr Dunne was a lawyer in the chambers of the then lord chief justice, Lord Goddard. Goddard and Greene were the supreme judicial authorities of their time and must have met at frequent intervals.

But this is mere conjecture, jury. Please weigh in your mind, the question of whether Mr Dunne, knowing so much, should have said so little. If he was pressed to acquiesce in the building of a narrative that would permit "security considerations" to be invoked at a time of wartime emergency, a man of his stamp would hardly refuse. Counsel asks you to weight the facts and decide: Was there a tacit agreement between Mr Dunne and Mr Macdonald Ross, for what they presumably felt to be the best of reasons, to bury the shocking truth? And, in the context of the resounding exclamations made in the commons by Mr Morrison about bringing out the truth behind the tragedy, does that amount to a conspiracy to mislead parliament and the nation? You may feel that in the circumstances these servants of the crown were faithfully doing what the minister and the cabinet required; or you may feel that there was a higher interest that needed to be served, and was not.

Let us now consider the testimony given to Mr Dunne by Mr William Joule Kerr, the regional technical adviser who thought measures to control the entry into the mouth of the shelter would be a waste of money.

It is possible, members of the jury, to detect a degree of testiness in Mr Dunne's questioning of this witness, a sterner, more accusatory tone which does not occur elsewhere in the inquiry; and we can be sure that Mr Kerr felt defensive and ill at ease. Let us look again at part of the transcript, at the point where the investigator asks: "Did you think that what you had sanctioned met the problem raised by the borough council?" Mr Kerr replies that "the problem they put in was from the lateral pressure from outside and I thought what I recommended was adequate for the pressure, preventing them breaking in from the sides."

Mr Dunne: "It did not occur to you that, in fact, the really vulnerable point was probably not the sides at all, but the front of the shelter?

"I recommended that the gates should be strengthened."

Mr Dunne: "Having what in mind?" "It was possible they might be closed or kept half-closed. Of course, in view of later events I see now that that would have been useless because they could not have closed them against the pressure of people."

Mr Dunne: "But Mr. Kerr that would be elementary would it not, you could not close a gate against a crowd of people?"

Mr Kerr: "No, I think not, if the people are under control."

Mr Dunne: "Yes, but what they are envisaging is people not under control. It is directly raised here, is it not? They are envisaging such a crowd of people as would cause the wooden structure to collapse?" "Yes."

The tenor of this conversation is not the same as the other exchanges; the difference, members of the jury, is that here is the man who realises that he might have grasped the peril that lurked on the staircase but did not and was now living with an uncomfortable awareness of terrible, irretrievable error. Counsel does not ask you to condemn Mr Kerr although you may do so in your verdict, if you are so minded. It has not been possible to find out what befell him after this episode but what happened at Bethnal Green suggests that his suitability for this kind of work might be questioned. As we know, the home front at this time was severely affected by manpower shortages; almost every able-bodied man from eighteen to forty-odd years had been swept into military service of one or another kind. If Mr Kerr survives somewhere until this day we must suppose that he is in his nineties at least. Perhaps he would come forward? There is much that he could tell.

Three of the players still visible in this drama remain to be considered: Mr Ian Macdonald Ross, Sir Ernest Gowers and Mr Morrison, later Lord Morrison of Lambeth.

Of Sir Ernest, there is much to admire; he was a notable civil servant with a distinguished career in the public service; after Rugby school and Clare college, Cambridge (a first in classics) he became principal private secretary to David Lloyd George at the treasury in 1911. Gowers went on to become chairman of the board of inland revenue and a campaigner for the use of clear and simple english. He took over as head of civil defence in London in 1940 when his predecessor, Admiral Edward Evans, was posted elsewhere.

Since Mr Dunne did not seek (or was not allowed) the opportunity to question Sir Ernest about his civil defence role, let's get what we can from other sources. By way of a first example here is part of the text of a letter from Sir Ernest to Mr Morrison on the evening of March 4, after the emergency meeting at Bethnal Green to consider what should be done to make the shelter safer. Sir Ernest writes

" ...that the object of the meeting was to ascertain the facts, to authorise any action immediately required and to discover whether there were any general lessons to be learned.

"The result was to confirm the conclusion to which we had come upon the statements obtained by the police, and other reports already available, and there was no difference of opinion among any of us as to the facts. .. We all agreed there were two main questions for consideration, viz:-

(a) whether by any structural improvement, the shelter could be made more secure against a similar disaster; and

(b) whether it was practicable to introduce any improvement of control of the public approaching the shelter.

"We decided to adjourn the discussion until the afternoon in order for these questions to be explored by the technical experts, while I discussed the latter with the commissioner of police.

The experts found no difficulty in reaching unanimous agreement on certain structural improvements which we hope to have completed in the very near future and I gave authority for the necessary work to be put in hand."

(Jury, as you already know, the 'structural improvements' comprised the introduction of a new ground-level entrance, via the adjacent Bethnal Green gardens, accessed past a crush barrier and a properly-lit covered pathway approach. This work represented a refined and more elaborate version of what the local council had been seeking.)

Contrast this direct and purposeful action with Sir Ernest's formal response to the Dunne report, a draft copy of which was sent to him by Sir Oswald Allen at the Home Office, three weeks later. He concurred in the suppression of the full report on the ground that it "would be too valuable a present to German propaganda".

He went on that it would be wrong to suppress Mr Dunne's exonerations of police and shelter wardens or the criticisms of London civil defence (which were in fact vague and extremely mild). Interestingly, Sir Ernest had nothing to say about the 'psychology' theory that was to be used to suppress the report. He only became animated when dealing with the question of whether Bethnal Green council or Mr Kerr had got it right over the danger on the staircase. You should ask yourselves, members of the jury, whether Sir Ernest, in his stout defence of his department, appears wilfully to misunderstand, or misrepresent, the thinking behind the ouncil's request. Here is what he says:

"As regards the criticism of London region, I think Mr Dunne fumbles a bit; I fancy what he is trying to say is something like this:

"The local authority wanted to substitute a brick wall for the wooden barrier because they were afraid that when the shelter got full it might be impossible to close it effectively to further entrants; the crowd might break down the barrier. The regional technical adviser thought that the expense of a brick wall was not justified because the wooden barrier could be so strengthened as to remove this fear. When the accident happened the shelter was not in fact full, the barrier did not in fact break, and there is no reason to suppose that the regional technical adviser was wrong.

"But this cannot be regarded as disposing of the matter. The local authority had made formal representations to the regional commissioner that there was a grave possibility, in certain circumstances, that a large number of shelterers would be precipitated down the staircase. They declared that, in the event of their proposals being rejected, the committee cannot accept any responsibility for the consequences which might ensue from the lack of adequate protection for the entrance to the shelter.

"So serious an issue having been raised, the comparatively junior administrative officer of London region , who, on the advice of the (regional technical adviser) rejected the local authority's request ought not to have taken it upon himself to accept this grave responsibility on behalf of the commissioners; the question ought to have been referred higher, perhaps even up to the principal officer.

"I think there some substance to this criticism and I feel bound, as the person responsible, to accept it. But to say this is not to say that the decision was wrong, or that that it would necessarily have been different if taken at a higher level; on the contrary, I think that, if it had come to me, I should probably have upheld the decision, knowing that this risk is inherent in all deep shelters approached by stairs and that this particular shelter had been safely used by thousands of people night after night during the worst of the London bombings."

To which Sir Oswald Allen replied, on April 2, saying the minister agreed that there should be a summary of conclusions for publication, "omitting the matter which would be of value to the enemy".

The minister naturally insisted, Sir Oswald wrote, that "in shortening the summary, there should be no risk of seeming to lighten the magistrate's criticisms of the local authority" (in fact Mr Dunne made no substantial criticism of the council) "or departmental administration).. against this, however, it can be said that the relatively full account to be presented gives the minister a better opportunity of defending his administration than a short version giving only the criticisms."

(Jury: There it is again! defending the administration? Where no fault is acknowledged, how arises the need for defence?

Sir Oswald then disclosed that the full report had been sent to the town clerk "with a copy of the official secrets act, giving authority for him to communicate its contents to the emergency committee and other individual councillors who may ask to see it, who will be liable to sanctions under the act if they make an unauthorised disclosure of the information contained in the report which will not be published in the summary of conclusions available to the public. The white paper containing the summary will be sent to the council with an official request for their observations. While the minister may have to say something about the report in parliament he would probably wish not to give his 'defence' until the local authorities were free to say what they wished on their own behalf."

Members of the jury you can see here the full beauty of the home office position and the subtlety of the burden imposed on the people in charge of the shelter. The councillors had a very sound knowledge of what had happened and what they had warned against. They did not need to be told by the ministry what had taken place but they were nonetheless force-fed the official narrative devised elsewhere, crushingly reminded of the terms of the official secrets act and in effect told: You are now parties to a state secret. Your lips are sealed.

Perhaps you may think it curious that the 'psychology' notion, of a flight to self-destruction as the enemy bombers draw near, does not figure at all in Sir Ernest's reply. Might it have been news to him that (allegedly) the morale of Londoners was fragmenting under the bombing? That would have been surprising; the blitz of 1940-41 had been much worse and this would have been an important new factor. But Sir Ernest did not even trouble to discuss it; all we see here is close attention to the defensive positioning of the ministry of home security and the regional commissioners. Note also to Sir Oswald's reference to the minister's "defence". What might have to be defended?

Neither of these officials touches upon the notion of a 'psychological' cause; the more substantial issues of the warnings that were ignored and the missing brick wall that was to be a crush barrier keep getting in the way. Each of these two will have noted Mr Dunne's comment in his report, in Paragraph 39 (e)

'...the absence of a crush barrier, allowing a straight line of pressure from the crowd seeking entrance to the people on the stairs. This was, in my opinion, the main structural defect at the time of the accident".

Sir Ernest strove to insist, despite the evidence, that his department's decision-making had not really failed and Sir Oswald Allen is eager to get the secrets act into play to shut down the story. Each official perceived that what the cabinet wanted and what the national interest required was secrecy. To that extent perhaps, we may acknowledge that they did what they thought best. But here is another insight (from file HO 186/2352) into what the civil defence boss was thinking about the organisation that he led, drawn from one of his regular quarterly reports to the minister, in January 1942 - just about the time that Stanley Ferdinando, the town clerk of Bethnal Green, was making a fourth application to make the staircase safer. Sir Ernest complained that his staff were becoming bored and restless and had come to believe that the war was nearly over:

"The task of maintaining the civil defence services in good heart does not get any easier as it becomes increasingly apparent that their decisive battle has been fought and won, and is not likely to be resumed in existing circumstances. Our difficulties have been further increased by the fact that the call up of the 10,000 people whom we have agreed to release is slower than we had expected. They have all received their papers and know that they are going; not unnaturally they have lost interest in civil defence work and are spreading the germs of indiscipline and disgruntlement.

"The most important problem for us remains, therefore, the joint one of preventing the services from rotting through idleness; and of harnessing their manpower to the present war effort. There is not much to be got out of the scheme for employing them on construction work, except perhaps, for a time, for the fire service.. After five weeks of effort, 24 men have been placed in factories under a system by which they work there for three weeks and then return to their depots for three weeks, and so on. The difficulties of fitting together the employers who want that sort of man and the men who want that sort of job have been formidable."

A month after Sir Ernest was writing this, Singapore fell to the Japanese; half a year later, Tobruk fell to the Afrika Korps; a year later, in January 1943, the Luftwaffe resumed heavy raids on London using far heavier bombs than had been seen in the first blitz. Peace and victory were a very long way further into the future than the civil defence mindset allowed for.

This spirit of complacency is reflected also in the actions of William Kerr who, when asked to approve building work at the mouth of the Bethnal Green shelter, thought no deeper about it than to ask the London passenger transport board if such a structure would be needed in peacetime. A copy of his letter reveals that he asked them – "Is it necessary?" It was his job, not theirs, to determine what was necessary for the safety of civilians under enemy attack. But when the tube people said no, he also said no. Fears for the safety of the civil population had given way to insistent calls for economy. The implication, members of the jury, is that London civil defence, or some parts thereof, thought they'd seen the worst the enemy could offer. But the Luftwaffe was not yet done with London and the V1 doodlebugs and the V2 rockets were still to come. To that extent, members of the jury, you may well feel that Sir Ernest and Mr Kerr can be judged to have been complacent.

Shall we now examine the actions of Mr Morrison in his presentation of the outcome of the Dunne report to the cabinet in April, 1943? We can wonder what it was that this clever, versatile politician really wanted from the cabinet. He is not on record as saying one way or the other. He'd set out the case for and against full disclosure and acknowledged that when the disaster surfaced the "discontented locals" at a public meeting had been held off only by a promise of a judge-led enquiry and full publication. He'd also warned that full disclosure would involve an impact "the effect on public morale through daily press reports of horrible details and suggestions of panic and fear".

Now with his master, Churchill, looking on, Mr Morrison discussed the release of material about the tragedy and mused whether it might be worse to stress the physical or the 'psychological' explanations. The latter would be the more dangerous, he warned, and added: "I can't use this report to protect the government". No-one needed to ask what needed protection; perhaps it was silently acknowledged around the cabinet table that there had been a bad blunder and that it must be concealed. As we have seen, the prime minister burst in to exclaim that he was against giving the limelight to such a matter; it would be meat and drink to the enemy. "Why publish?" he demanded. "The government's position is unassailable". Of course it was; the government's commons majority was enormous; the press was under control; the critics could never make their case.

"It says there was panic" Mr Churchill declared. He was right to the extent that, indeed, the words were there on the pages of the report, there was the evidence, or maybe merely testimony, for the psychology theory and so the state secret – a legend of civilian panic and cowardice - was safely born. The investigator had spoken (or appeared to have spoken) and that was good enough. It did not count, perhaps, that all but twenty-seven of the 173 victims had been women and children. They had, so it was said, lost their self-control and that was a shameful secret the enemy must not be allowed to glimpse. The conjuring trick that had emerged from the ministry of home security dazzled the cabinet and it did not care to look deeper, to see how it was done. They did not ask to hear the words spoken by the witnesses at the tribunal, nor would they have wanted to. There was a war to be won and they were busy people.

But unlike them we now can take the time to wonder who it was that wove those words into Mr Dunne's tapestry or, as the minister himself put it, "changed Mr Dunne's language". And to wonder also who was the master and who the servant in the relationship between Mr Dunne and Mr Macdonald Ross.

In our time, members of the jury, in our calm and peaceful time, an investigation into such a disaster would demand an inquisitor with the standing of a high court judge at least. And the judge's official assistants at such an investigation would be clearly separated from the ministry under scrutiny – drawn perhaps from the treasury or the cabinet office, or the civil service department.

Instead the documents you have seen will show that the inquiry was skewed towards a finding that would clear Mr Morrison's department. If the bad news got out, it would have been a scandal that would surely cost the minister his job and his reputation. He had the responsibility, even though, of course, he was personally blameless; what had happened was something that he as minister, could not possibly have prevented. We can agree, jury, that to that extent Mr Morrison could not be convicted of blame for the disaster; not even for the civil defence failings; they were all in place before he'd taken over; in the same way, Mr Macdonald Ross was the servant who brought to fruition what his master had prescribed; a misty conjecture of how it might profit the enemy to learn of some alleged and elusive psychological weakness. Did anyone believe it? Almost certainly not but it served for the time. Were they right to perpetuate it? Let us agree, ladies and gentlemen of the jury, that it suffices we know at last something like the truth about what happened at Bethnal Green and accept that it is conceivable that a public relations disaster was averted.

Even so there is another, graver charge to be brought against Mr Morrison, one that cannot be explained away by the pressures of wartime necessity; the test came later, when with victory in sight, it was possible for the ministry to be open and transparent; to allow it to be admitted that subterfuge had been adopted in the matter of the Bethnal Green shelter. He did not take this opportunity; faced with probing questions in the commons he contrived to deflect and prolong the concealment and thereby caused the course of justice to be perverted. I refer here again to the matter of the civil action brought by Annie Baker which led, against all reason, to a judgment that the council had been negligent.

# CHAPTER 10
## Missing, Believed Destroyed

By a curious coincidence both Herbert Morrison and the metropolitan borough of Bethnal Green passed away in the same year, 1965. The council fell victim to local government reorganisation which decreed that to be small and accessible was inefficient. Thus Bethnal Green became part of Tower Hamlets. The disappearance of Bethnal Green council possibly explains the absence of some of the wartime records it kept – those which could have demonstrated that, in its administration of the tube shelter, it had not been negligent.

Counsel sought enlightenment from its successor, the London borough of Tower Hamlets and there eventually emerged a collection of papers which can be viewed at the Bancroft Road library, near Stepney Green tube station. There are a couple of important artefacts, one a book of Bethnal Green council minutes which records the emergency committee in August 1941 as follows:

RESOLVED: (1) That the regional commissioners be informed that, in the opinion of the committee, strong protection to the entrance to the tube shelter was both urgent and necessary, having regard to the need to prevent, in the event of heavy attack from the air, an abnormal influx of persons seeking shelter therein.

This was the trigger for Stanley Ferdinando, the town clerk, to write to the regional commissioners and it is almost all that remains of the council's attempt to make safe the shelter staircase. There are no copies to be found at the Bancroft Rd library of the town clerk's four letters to the regional commissioners about the mouth of the shelter (or at least they had not surfaced when counsel made searches). They exist only in the ministry of home security papers at Kew.

Is this not indeed extraordinary, members of the jury, that these letters, and the reports of the Baker case and the Appeal Court hearing are all that remains of the matter? Counsel has passed many days at the national archives at Kew, has trawled exhaustively among government papers on a multitude of matters; here and there are gleams of gold, but there is also much dross. It would be expected that a high court case such as that between Mrs Annie Baker and Bethnal Green corporation should have a full official record but it appears there is none. It has been destroyed. Counsel has searched, so far as is allowed, at the national archives but the papers do not come to light. Counsel enquired further; nobody knows where they are – or, indeed, papers of other comparable actions of the Kings Bench division of the period..

A request was made to the ministry of justice, as successor to the home office, under the freedom of information act; may we see the case papers from the trial or any correspondence relating to it between the home office, or the ministry of home security and the office of the attorney general? (It will be recalled that the attorney-general intervened in the case to have the trial heard in camera.)

The request was answered from the royal courts of justice, a spokeswoman for which replied that "Her majesty's court service does not hold this information. Files and court records are destroyed in accordance with our file and records retention policy and schedules. Case files in the court of appeal are destroyed three years after the date of the last action."

Pressed to clarify this excessive zeal in housekeeping, the spokeswoman wrote: "The file about a case belongs to the court, not to the parties to the proceedings, nor to any other interested parties. Therefore the court, under the authority of the departmental tecords officer, can destroy its file once sufficient time has elapsed since the last action to be taken by any party to the proceedings, if such files are not to be permanently preserved".

Members of the jury might reasonably suppose that case papers from the Kings Bench division were not really the property of the court at all but of the crown, from whence the court's authority derives; and you might wonder, in view of this, what constitutes a ground for a file to be permanently preserved? Here was a case revolving around the worst civilian disaster of the war, a terrible toll of lives, a case spectacularly exceptional in that a civil lawsuit was heard only in secret, and one that, in its aftermath, brought down scathing judicial criticism upon the home secretary; also a case which eventually involved a very substantial outlay of public money, secretly disbursed via a small local authority. What would constitute grounds for permanent preservation if not this? How could such a dossier be consigned to the furnace as something not interesting or instructive to future generations? But it seems certain that these court papers, and many others from the war period, were destroyed, and on the authority of a senior judge, Lord Denning, a year or so before the death of Lord Morrison.

But we must press on, we have the outline of the matter. We know anyway that Mrs Baker won her lawsuit and in his judgment Mr Justice Singleton decided Bethnal Green corporation had been negligent. Without the heavy fist of the official secrets act brought into play, the council could have shown that it had been farseeing rather than negligent and that when it strove to improve the safety of the staircase it had been officially thwarted. The minister who was responsible both for shelter safety and the integrity of the law, being one and the same person, and in full knowledge of this, took steps only to prevent the truth from coming out.

As we know, the council appealed against Mr Justice Singleton's judgment and this was heard in December, 1944, by the master of the rolls, Lord Justice Greene. Counsel asks your indulgence, members of the jury, to be repetitious here, to revisit earlier ground because this is a significant plank in the prosecution case, the strictures of Lord Greene.

As you may recall, he observed that it was perfectly proper for Mr Justice Singleton to allow the request by the attorney general for the case to go ahead in secret, remarking that "in practice he could do nothing else" and accepting that the attorney-general also had acted properly in making the application "on instructions". But then Lord Greene added that it was unfortunate that the instruction had been given. The present case was one which led to a critical examination of what a public authority had done in performing its duty to the public and in which, conceivably, some officials of the ministry might have been subject to some kind of criticism. If ever there was a case where evidence should have been given in open court, this was such a case. "Although the ministry thought that the grounds on which they acted were solid grounds, they were of the flimsiest description."

We can rejoice that the Appeal Court so squarely demolished Mr Morrison's subterfuge. But it has to be admitted that neither justice nor Bethnal Green corporation benefited; the Singleton verdict remained substantially in place, as it does to this day. The matter has not been put right. Mr Morrison was allowed to brazen it out in the house of commons and so the matter has fallen into a sort of deep-freeze.

The web that was woven within the ministry of home security held fast; no-one could disentangle what was true, what mattered and why; Bethnal Green Council was silenced by threats, saddled with the blame and ignominy of a shocking catastrophe, the stolid and stoic people of the east end who had endured, along with so many others, the frightful carnage of the blitz, were defamed as cowards who had cracked under the bombings. Meanwhile the taxpayer, as usual, picked up the bill, no questions asked. The minister of the crown who had said: "The parliamentary responsibility is undoubtedly fully mine, and I accept it" did quite the opposite.

As we have seen, Mr Morrison did not appear in the commons when the moment arrived, on January 19, 1945, for him to make a parliamentary statement about the shelter disaster. The outcome of the war was no longer in the slightest doubt and there was no justification (if there ever had been) for concealment. Nonetheless he sent word of a medical emergency and Sir John Anderson appeared in his place, as we have seen. No disclosure was made that would have absolved or lightened the burden of blame upon the councillors of the borough of Bethnal Green.

At the same time the Dunne report was placed in the vote office and summaries of (parts of) what it said were made available to the media. The story was thus revealed, or might we say emitted, in the papers of January 20, 1945, on the lines laid down in the home office summary offered to the war cabinet. Fragments of the 'psychology' theory were aired again - "a strong apprehension of drastic reprisals" by the Luftwaffe, "a sudden rush for the entrance" and "the absence of a crush barrier". Nothing was now said about the infantile notion that

German bombers might exploit the alleged hysterical terror of the civilian population fleeing to shelter. Nowadays, of course, the release of such a document as the Dunne report would have been the signal for reporters to swarm around the locality, seeking explanations and reactions. But in those straitened times, that did not happen; news stories had to be compressed rather than expanded and developed; and anyway, of course, those councillors and officials were still bound by the official secrets act. The world moved swiftly on and the anguish of Bethnal Green, like so many other wartime traumas, slipped out of sight.

So jury, knowing what we now know, how should we judge Mr Morrison and his aide, Mr Macdonald Ross and the other, less visible creatures of the home office and the ministry for home security? It has been impossible to flesh out Mr Macdonald Ross; nothing is traceable beyond his appearances in the pages you have seen, (although perhaps there are personnel documents that await release).

We can only wonder how and why he could say, in his guidance notes to Mr Dunne, that "accidental collapse of crowd without panic owing to fall of woman near foot of stairs" was a false explanation for the tragedy. The words were in his own handwriting. Mr Macdonald Ross had sat through the tribunal hearings, had heard the harrowing, terrible stories, the evidence of the engineers and the shelter wardens. The fall of the elderly woman was, without question, the trigger for what happened in that lethally confined space. As Walter Steadman and Eliza Jones reported – and we can be sure they spoke the truth – this woman and the little boy lost their footing - and their lives - and most of those behind and above her on the staircase lost theirs too, with the result that we know.

It was Mr Macdonald Ross also, who we see to have been insistently pressing the word 'panic' upon Mr Dunne, in the face of what was being said by the calm and stolid police officers, the wardens and the shelterers. Even the master of the rolls, in the appeal court, joined the chorus: "It was perfectly well-known that there had been no panic". Maybe we should agree, jury, that Mr Macdonald Ross served his master well and leave it to that.

Mr Morrison has published several books about his life and career and although they do not nowadays make for very lively reading, his life was indeed remarkable. He was certainly a most able politician, although that is not necessarily a compliment. For a cabinet minister, his beginnings, from 1888, were highly unusual and unpromising; he was one of several children born to Henry and Priscilla Morrison, at Brixton in south London; she had been a domestic servant, he was a police constable. 'Bert' as Lord Morrison of Lambeth was first known, lost an eye through infection in early childhood. He was educated at local state schools, started work in a shop then became a switchboard operator and then a newspaper circulation representative, before joining the London labour movement and rising rapidly. At twenty-seven he was secretary of the London labour party and in the first, short-lived labour government he served as transport minister. He was generally identified as pragmatic, forceful and persuasive. It is helpful to know this because in 1939, a few months before war was declared, Mr Morrison, in his capacity as leader of the London county council, was heading a delegation of all local authorities to Sir John Anderson, chancellor of the exchequer in the Chamberlain government. They were trying to settle the complexities of what the government wanted local councils to pay for if and when war broke out, including the provision of air raid shelters, fire services and the evacuation of children. A lengthy account of the confrontation survives in a home security file, HO 186/52.

It is interesting as an illustration of Mr Morrison's fluent and incisive advocacy and his powerful grasp of local authority imperatives; but it would be a digression to quote from it. Let it suffice that it shows Mr Morrison's effortless grasp of the way the system worked between local councillors and their officials, and between town hall and Whitehall. As the possessor of such knowledge, and cast in the model of a man of the people, one might think Mr Morrison would have been gracious and sympathetic in the hour of Bethnal Green's need. But instead the impression that arises from the dossiers at Kew is one of machiavellian ruthlessness. Perhaps it is naive to suppose other statesmen might be otherwise.

So who, if any, should be cast as villains? We can easily agree that criminals were principally to blame for the destruction and carnage in the east end and elsewhere and that these were the madmen in Berlin, Adolf Hitler, Goebbels, Himmler, Goering and the others. Their actions created the situation which led to the fatal crush on the staircase; but we cannot blame the nazis for not troubling themselves about protecting British civilians; that was the task of the Crown, the Crown which had given security guarantees to Poland which it could not possibly honour, the same Crown which declared war upon Germany when it was only too manifestly not equipped to wage such a war. You may recall that Mr Macdonald Ross, in his potted history of the civil defence organisation, remarked that in the early days, as war drew near, there was "a great deal of slit-trench provision". By that he meant people were put to work digging six-foot holes in the ground for the population to stand in while bombs fell around them. Here is the true, magnificent indifference of the British system, the imperial echo, members of the jury, of the Great War mentality, in which the infantry marches to the slaughter because those directing the nation's affairs cannot be trusted, or are perhaps unable, to put the lives of their ordinary countrymen above delusions of glory.

In this connection, it seems appropriate to mention a telling phrase that slips into the discourse of Sir Ernest Gowers in his reports to the minister about the progress of civil defence in 1942. The first phase of the blitz is over, the destructive fury of the Luftwaffe has been redirected towards Soviet Russia and some kind of lull in the hostilities seems to have taken hold. The authorities begin to fret that some thousands of Londoners are still going down into the deep tube shelters to sleep overnight. The suggestion was made, Sir Ernest records, "that these remaining limpets should be moved into the new deep shelters, and persons should be forbidden to spend the night in stations used for traffic. I think there is a case for clearing out the tube limpets ..."

In case there are some among you, jury, who have never visited a rocky seashore, a limpet is a cone-shaped mollusc notable for its ability to cling steadfastly to a rock surface, resisting all attempts to prise it loose. It is a clever, witty, heartless metaphor, to liken those Londoners who suffered trauma, homelessness and loss to limpets. You may feel that it smacks of arrogance and insensitivity. But it is very much in the vein of Mr Dunne's breezy "good old cockney" observations during his conversation with superintendent Hill, in which the working people of the east end become somehow akin to characters drawn from musical comedy.

Perhaps you may feel, members of the jury, that counsel is digressing here, has strayed from the case for the prosecution and the goal of identifying those to be blamed and punished. But we have to understand the official mindset, what it was that led to the staircase disaster.

Counsel puts it to you that there was complacency and negligence; the official view, encapsulated in Churchill's remark – "What notice is taken of those who died in air attacks?" bespeaks an attitude that at this time, human life was there to be squandered; it did not much matter if people might die, one way or another, on a dark staircase at Bethnal Green because they were just a few among the multitude; this was war and people got killed anywhere, soldiers in battle, refugee columns, bomber crews, merchant seamen.

If you subscribe to this view, you may very well accept that the minister for home security, the head of London civil defence, Mr Ian Macdonald Ross and Mr William Joule Kerr acted rightly and reasonably.

But then perhaps, as your head sinks on the pillow and the night closes around you, you might still find that in the darkness you are facing the pale, frightened little faces of the children and their hurrying, anxious fathers and mothers of Bethnal Green, who had no reason to die on that night of March 3, 1943, and, in their pointless death, were defamed by the lie that they "lost their self-control" and that "no forethought in the matter of structural improvement" on the staircase could have made any difference.

And you will have to explain to yourself why the councillors and corporation of the London borough of Bethnal Green, having conscientiously striven to make the staircase safer, were then convicted of negligence by a judge who heard only what the guilty party, the minister and servants of the Crown, decided he should hear. And you may wish to hear an answer to the mystery: Were the records of the 1944 trial and the subseequent appeal destroyed, and why? And if not, where are they now?

What say you, members of the jury? Guilty? Or not guilty?

# CHAPTER 11
## By Way of a Postscript

Like the archives at Bethnal Green, home office and home security papers about the tragedy have been extensively purged of any frank and revealing evaluation of what took place. But not everything was successfully "sanitized". Because of the steady drizzle of compensation payments to the bereaved, Treasury departments were also involved. Ponder on these fragments of a letter from Arthur Edmunds of the ministry of home security to a treasury colleague, E C Lester on October 7, 1943

"your letter about expenditure being incurred on measures to control entry into large public shelters...in the case of Bethnal Green the figure quoted is in respect of works put in hand within twenty-four hours of the disaster, when the situation was such as to make immediate action essential. This does not mean that we were stampeded into unduly extensive or costly measures.

"What looks like the relatively high cost at Bethnal Green is largely, if not wholly, explained by the fact that this shelter is unique in comparison with similar shelters of equal capacity in having only one entrance, a state of affairs which results in the congregation of a considerable crowd seeking admission on the occasion of an alert.

"The steps we have taken have been directed to ensuring that this crowd can only approach the entrance in the form of an orderly queue instead of an unregulated mob and to affording this queue adequate head cover and lateral protection during the interval which must necessarily elapse before they actually enter the shelter.

"You will ask, not unnaturally, whether the provision of a second entrance would not meet the case, but Mr. Dunne, who held the official inquiry, emphatically pronounced against this on the ground that it would merely transfer the risk of a further calamity to the booking hall by creating a dangerous congestion at the head of the escalators ..

"Bethnal Green council ... are still very "jittery" and our relations with them are decidedly strained owing to what they regard as the unhelpful and unsympathetic attitude we have adopted in respect of the legal proceedings against them ... I attended meetings of the emergency committee ... and I can honestly say that I have never been called upon to deal with a more truculent or uncompromising body nor felt so completely uncomfortable!

"You will. appreciate, I think, that the Bethnal Green shelter is in fact potentially more dangerous than the others (I think I am right in saying that the Southwark tunnel to which you refer has no less than seven entrances; and I have not the slightest doubt that we have succeeded in keeping down the remedial works undertaken and consequently the cost to public funds to the lowest practicable limit..."

# APPENDIX A
# Tube Shelter Disaster – The Victims
## List of persons killed

| | | |
|---|---|---|
| Aarons, Betty | 14 years | 10 Crescent house, E2 |
| Asser, Jesse | 33 | 44 Newcourt House E2 |
| Baker, George | 38 | 43 Braintree St E2 |
| Baker, Minnie | 14 | 43 Braintree St E2 |
| Bailey, Mary | 72 | 27 Whitman House, E2 |
| Bailey, Rose | 41 | 27 Whitman Hse, E2 |
| Bars, Eileen | 7 | 39 Portman Place E2 |
| Beaken, Ethel Louisa | 53 | 29 Morris House, E2 |
| Beaken, Eileen Louisa | 17 | 29 Morris House, E2 |
| Beaken, Matilda Jane | 40 | 70 Handley Road, E9 |
| Berger, Emily Jemima | 57 | 12 Stainsbury Street, E1 |
| Bendon, Elizabeth | 38 | 73 Cyprus St, E2 |
| Bennett, Emma Maud | 48 | 15 Moore House E2 |
| Bosworth, Irene Patricia | 17 | 10 Burnham Estate, E2 |
| Bosworth, Edith | 50 | 10 Burnham Estate, E2 |
| Boxer, Annie | 24 | 20 Hunslett St E2 |
| Brooks, Henry Norman | 10 | 11 Swinburne House, E2 |
| Brooks, Jessie | 46 | 11 Swinburne House, E2 |
| Brookstone, Israel | 67 | 41 Teesdale Street, E2 |
| Bowling, Bessie | 59 | 1 Milton House, E2 |
| Bowling, Eliza | 31 | 1 Milton House, E2 |
| Butterfield, Allan | 3 | 149 Corfield Street, E2 |
| Butterfield, George | 28 | 149 Corfield Street, E2 |
| Butterfield, Lottie | 28 | 149 Corfield Street, E2 |
| Chandler, Doreen Mary | 14 | 21 Burnham Estate, E2 |
| Chandler, Lilian Mary | 35 | 21 Burnham Estate, E2 |
| Chapman, Charlotte Elizabeth | 25 | 21 Hersee Place, E2 |
| Chapman, George James | 25 | 17 Swinburne House, E2 |
| Clatworthy, Iris | 2 | 156 Bancroft Road, E2 |

| | | |
|---|---|---|
| Clatworthy, Joan | 9½ | 156 Bancroft Road, E2 |
| Coleman, Maud Louisa | 54 | 236 Globe Road, E2 |
| Collett, Doreen | 11 | 9 Stainsbury Street E1 |
| Collett, Rose | 50 | 9 Stainsbury Street E1 |
| Collett, Ronald | 8 | 9 Stainsbury Street E1 |
| Colman, Richard Trueman | 34 | 12 Whitman House, E2 |
| Court, Patricia Marie | 24 | 6 Electric House, E3 |
| Day, John Lewis | 69 | 6 Gawber Street, E2 |
| Dongrey, Annie | 22 | 33 Bandon Road, E2 |
| Ellam, Rosina Ellen | 17 | 31 Wessex Street, E2 |
| Ellam, Annie Eva | 44 | 31 Wessex Street, E2 |
| Ellam, Frances Lilian | 20 | 31 Wessex Street, E2 |
| Ellam, Pauline | 2½ | 31 Wessex Street, E2 |
| Emery, Clara | 78 | 41 Hollybush Gdns, E2 |
| Ewett, Ivy | 23 | 1 Digby Street, E2 |
| Fletcher, Alexander | 3 | 334 Corfield Street, E2 |
| Fletcher, Elizabeth | 28 | 334 Corfield Street, E2 |
| Forbes, Leonora | 57 | 27 Bishops Way, E2 |
| Forbes, Irene Catherine | 17 | 27 Bishops Way, E2 |
| Fowler, Mary Ann | 45 | 42 Gawber Street, E2 |
| French, Lilian | 29 | 73 Cyprus Street, E2 |
| Geary, Carole Ann | 5 months | 9 Peary Place, E2 |
| Geary, Sylvia Sadie | 6 years | 9 Peary Place, E2 |
| Grover, Ethel | 48 | 302 Globe Road, E2 |
| Hall, Edna Phoebe | 13 | 148 Mansford Street, E2 |
| Hall, Annie Jessie | 52 | 148 Mansford Street, E2 |
| Hall, Irene | 8 | 17 Burnham Estate, E2 |
| Hall, Mary Ann | 47 | 17 Burnham Estate, E2 |
| Hales, Joe | 53 | 8 Crossland Square, E2 |
| Hammond, Rhoda | 44 | 18 Approach Road, E2 |
| Harris, Olive Margaret | 17 | 86 Royston Street, E2 |
| Hayman, Mary Ann | 19 | 26 Burnham Estate, E2 |
| Hawley, Leonard Joseph | 64 | 143 Antill Road, E3 |
| Higginson, Emily | 62 | 10 Seabright Street E2 |
| Hillier, Mary Ann | 61 | 3 Kirkwall Place, E2 |
| Hiscocke, Ivy | 22 | 65 Gretton House, E2 |
| Hoye, Lilian | 13 | 106 Roman Road, E2 |
| Hoye, Marjorie | 7 | 106 Roman Road, E2 |
| Hoye, Louisa | 44 | 106 Roman Road, E2 |
| Hoye, Rose | 19 | 106 Roman Road, E2 |
| Hutchinson, Joan Peggy | 10 | 16 Bonwell Street, E2 |
| Hutchinson, William George | 6 | 16 Bonwell Street, E2 |
| Ingle, Agnes Maud | 28 | 247 Globe Road, E2 |
| Johnson, Caroline Ivy | 14 | 11 Holly Mansions, E2 |
| Johnson, Helen Emma | 6 | 11 Holly Mansions, E2 |
| Jolly, Sarah | 51 | 41 Burnham Estate, E2 |
| Johns, Peter | 7½ | 41 Burnham Estate, E2 |
| Jones, Estella | 57 | 33 Old Ford Road, E2 |
| Juilier, Henry | 18 | 91 Bishops Way, E2 |

| | | |
|---|---|---|
| Korobenic, Eliza | 33 | 66 Newcourt House, E2 |
| Land, Barbara | 7 | 1 Bullards Place, E2 |
| Land, Martha Elizabeth | 56 | 43 Monteith Road, E3 |
| Lapham, Ronald | 15 | 10 Approach Road, E2 |
| Lawson, Anthony William | 7 | 172 Roman Road, E2 |
| Lawson, Patricia Eileen | 3 | 172 Roman Road, E2 |
| Lazarus, Maurice | 42 | 157 Bethnal Green Rd. |
| Letchmere, Florence Rosetta | 66 | 3 Entick Street, E2 |
| Letchmere, Thomas Allen | 48 | 19 Entick Street, E2 |
| Letchmere, Thomas | 66 | 3 Entick Street, E2 |
| Leggett, Benjamin George | 31 | 16 Bandon Road, E2 |
| Leggett, Rose Maud | 31 | 16 Bandon Road, E2 |
| Leggett, Roy Benjamin | 7 | 16 Bandon Road, E2 |
| Lewis, George Ronald | 10 | 10 Moore House, E2 |
| Lewis, Lilie Elizabeth | 14 | 10 Moore House, E2 |
| Loftus, John Samuel | 13 | 32 Grendon House, E2 |
| Loftus, Louisa Ellen | 15 | 32 Grendon House, E2 |
| Maguire, Jean Mary | 9 | 28 Butler Estate, E2 |
| Mason, Charles | 50 | 20 Russia Lane E2 |
| Mathers, Ruby | 18 | 116 Beale Road, E3 |
| Mead, Eliza | 67 | 66 Newcourt House, E2 |
| Mead, Florence | 35 | 7 Peary Place, E2 |
| Mead, George | 40 | 7 Peary Place, E2 |
| Mead, George | 12 | 7 Peary Place, E2 |
| Mead, Maureen | 4 | 7 Peary Place, E2 |
| Mead, Kenneth | 10 | 7 Peary Place, E2 |
| Morris, Derek | 6 | 25 Montfort House, E2 |
| Morris, Florence Maud | 30 | 25 Montfort House, E2 |
| Myers, Jeffrey | 6 | 55 Cleveland Way, E1 |
| Neville, Alfred | 45 | 42 Gawber Street, E2 |
| Newman, Doris | 9 | 24 Tagg Street, E2 |
| Newman, George | 45 | 24 Tagg Street, E2 |
| Newton, Sarah Ann | 28 | 25 Wessex Street, E2 |
| Nixon, William Henry | 14 | 7 Burns House, E2 |
| Papworth, Rosina | 27 | 80 Morpeth Street, E2 |
| Patterson, Mary | 44 | 8 Brierly Street, E2 |
| Perryment, Iris | 17 | 74 Morpeth Street, E2 |
| Poole, Sarah | 54 | 87 Mansford St. Bldgs |
| Price, Rose Elizabeth | 27 | 37 Viaduct Street, E2 |
| Pusey, Emily | 48 | 7 Shelley House, E2 |
| Pusey, Henry | 50 | 7 Shelley House, E2 |
| Quorn, Emily Elizabeth | 43 | 5 Peel Grove, E2 |
| Quorn, Gwendoline Mary | 5 | 5 Peel Grove, E2 |
| Quorn, William Frederick | 14 | 5 Peel Grove, E2 |
| Raulinaitis, Joseph | 32 | 9 Hammond Gdns, E2 |
| Redwin, Eileen Margaret | 7 | 236 Globe Road, E2 |
| Relf, Rose Lilian (Jnr) | 13 | 192 Wilmot Street, E2 |
| Relf, Rose Lilian | 41 | 192 Wilmot Street, E2 |
| Reynolds, George Francis | 72 | 239 Camb HeathRd.E2 |

| Riddell, Stella | 13 | 51 Burnham Estate, E2 |
| Ridgeway, Ellen | 28 | 24 Brierly Street, E2 |
| Roche, Bessie | 42 | 123 Canrobert Street, E2 |
| Roche, Eddie | 8 | 123 Canrobert Street, E2 |
| Roche, Joan | 9 | 123 Canrobert Street, E2 |
| Roche, Ted | 40 | 123 Canrobert Street, E2 |
| Seabrooke, Sarah Florence | 62 | 163 Gretton House, E2 |
| Seabrooke, Barry James | 3 | 163 Gretton House, E2 |
| Sears, William Herbert | 50 | 15 Patriot Square, E2 |
| Sharpe, Irene | 16 months | |
| Sharpe, Kenneth | 4 | |
| *(both of 5 Kings Flats, Maidstone, Kent, staying at 20 Kerbela Street, E2)* | | |
| Sheperd, Arthur Theodore | 42 | 19 Model Bldgs. Kings X |
| Smith, Dorothy Ann | 12 | 9 Roman Road, E2 |
| Sceats, Lilian Doris | 15 | 31 Whitman House, E2 |
| Speight, Edith Margaret | 47 | 9 Horwood House, E2 |
| Sinnocks, Lydia Elizabeth | 62 | 6 Morpeth Street, E2 |
| Spicer, Joan Pamela | 5 | 10 Bonwell Street, E2 |
| Spicer, Tony Anthony Edwin | 9 | 10 Bonwell Street, E2 |
| Stevens, Mary Anne Elizabeth | 55 | 36a Waterloo Gardens, E2 |
| Stretch, Rose | 39 | 159 Wilmot Street, E2 |
| Stretch, William | 9 | 159 Wilmot Street, E2 |
| Tarbuck, George | 45 | 63 Newcourt House, E2 |
| Tarbuck, Louisa | 44 | 63 Newcourt House, E2 |
| Taylor, Sarah | 54 | 27 Wessex Street, E2 |
| Taylor, James William | 12 | 10 Lansdell Place, E2 |
| Thompson, Kate | 53 | 83 Quinns Square, E2 |
| Thorpe, Barbara | 2 | 20 Kerbela Street, E2 |
| Thorpe, Marie | 11 | 20 Kerbela Street, E2 |
| Thorpe, Olive | 36 | 20 Kerbela Street, E2 |
| Tilbury, Clara Selina | 49 | 31 Burnham Estate, E2 |
| Trayling, Irene Lilian | 20 | 9 Kirkwall Place, E2 |
| Trice, Isabella Rose | 39 | 42 Wessex Street, E2 |
| Trotter, Lilian Maud | 36 | 26 Morpeth Street, E2 |
| Trotter, Vera Lilian | 7 | 26 Morpeth Street, E2 |
| Vann, Maud | 23 | 74 Hadrian Estate, E2 |
| Vanner, Florence Eliza | 49 | 68 Burnham Estate, E2 |
| Warrington, Doris Beatrice | 16 | 62 Blythe Street, E2 |
| Welch, James | 52 | 37 Digby Estate, E2 |
| Whitehead, James Henry | 69 | 6 Viaduct Street, E2 |
| Wilson, Edna Rosina | 15 | 37 Butler Estate, E2 |
| Wood, Alfred William | 60 | 5 Kenilworth Road, E2 |
| Woolnough, Elsie Hilda | 37 | 35 Mansford Bldg. E2 |
| Woolnough, Alice Elsie | 12 | 35 Mansford Building E2 |
| Yeaman, John Robert Charles | 1 | 5 Peel Grove, E2 |

Total number of persons 173

(Author's note: The location of the accident and names, ages and addresses of the victims were not published at the time, for reasons of wartime secrecy. In the same way, so far as was possible, families were left to bury their own dead. This is the list compiled by the Metropolitan Police and in some cases differences arise with other lists assembled by relatives.)

# APPENDIX B
# The Dunne Report

Here follow some fragments of the Dunne Report. The original can be found in the British Library but is not now generally available for purchase. It was priced at seven shillings and sixpence and, theoretically could be bought at HMSO after 1945 although just how many did so is a moot point. This summary is taken from the draft version surviving on a home office file so detail differences may exist between this and the published version. The alternative versions have not been compared.

Mr Dunne begins by saying his tribunal sat from the 11th to the 17th of March and heard 80 witnesses. He notes that the entrance to the staircase

"is wider than the stairs. ...They are plain rough concrete steps with a square wooden insertion on the edge of the tread. They are fairly level though the wooden edge is worn a little below the level of the concrete. The walls of the stairway are wooden with brick piers and support an iron roof, a wooden hand rail attached to each wall, a bulkhead light on the ceiling vertically over the sixth step from the bottom".

" The only lighting of this stair came from a 25 watt lamp in the bulkhead light fixed in the ceiling, which was completely obscured save for a narrow slit of far from clear glass. The cone of the light emitted was adjusted as far as possible to strike the edge of the first step down and to give a dim light ..

" The shelter .. was opened early in October, 1940. . has a total bunked accommodation of something over 5,000, with additional shelter for another 5,000, only one entrance, though there is an emergency exit some half a mile away. It was and is the largest single unit of deep shelter in the whole area, and provides a greater proportion of deep shelter per head of population than in any of the adjoining boroughs. From its opening it was used by large numbers nightly during the period of intensive bombing, 1940-1941. Since the summer of 1941 the regular users have dwindled from some thousands nightly to a mere 200-300.

"News was received on March 2 of our heavy raid on Berlin and on that night 850 people actually used the shelter. Again many people were seen in the neighbourhood of the shelter in the streets, obviously up to a late hour prepared to use the shelter if an alert was sounded. The general expectation, however, seems from my inquiries to have been that a reprisal attack was far more likely to be launched on the 3rd

" On the night of March 3 the alert sounded at 8.17 p.m. precisely. By this time it was estimated that about 500-600 people were already in the shelter. The gates had all been opened some time prior to the alert. The chances of a raid were freely discussed but the people were perfectly orderly and normal in the manner of their entry up to the time of the sounding of the alert. Immediately the alert was sounded a large number of people left their homes in the utmost haste for the shelter. A great many were running. Two cinemas at least in the near vicinity disgorged a large number of people and at least three omnibuses set down their passengers outside the shelter. From 8.17 and for the next ten minutes there was a hurried convergence of hundreds of people towards, and at, the gates of the shelter. The people were nervous and anxious to get under cover. The entrance of the shelter was densely packed though there was no actual disorder, and the people were able to enter the shelter in a hurried but orderly stream.

"As fast as they passed down the stairs, numbers were converging at the entrance behind them. In the ten minutes succeeding the alert it is estimated that some 1,500 people entered the shelter. A number of these had had advance warning before the actual alert from the fact that their relay wireless had gone off. This, apparently, is a nearly certain sign that an alert will follow. The proportion of women and children was large. At this time there was gunfire, but it was distant and, according to numerous witnesses, not very alarming. No bombs or other missiles had fallen within a radius of some miles of the shelter.

" At precisely 8.27 p.m. a salvo of [anti-aircraft] rockets was discharged from a battery some third of a mile away. This caused a great deal of alarm. Some people on their way to the shelter lay down in the road and then ran on. There were some cries reported that "they were starting dropping them" or that a land mine [was seen descending] and other alarming observations. The crowd surged forward towards the entrance carrying in front of it those who were entering the shelter, and placing a severe and sudden pressure upon the backs of those already descending the nearly dark stairway.

10. Either as a result of this sudden pressure from behind, or, by an unlucky coincidence simultaneously with the pressure reaching the people immediately behind her, a woman, said to have been holding or leading a child, fell on the third step from the bottom. This was observed both by a witness on the landing below and by at least two people in the crowd on the stairs behind her. As a result or, again, simultaneously, a man fell on her left. This occurred in the right hand half of the stairway. So great was the pressure from behind that those impeded by the bodies were forced down on top of them with their heads outwards and towards the landing. In a matter of seconds there was built an immovable and interlaced mass of bodies five or six or more deep against which the people above and on the stairs continued to be forced by the pressure from behind.

"I have not been able to establish definitely whether the woman's fall was fortuitous or caused by pressure. I think there is little doubt that it was the latter. The evidence of a Mrs. Barber who witnessed the fall from behind seems to show that she, Mrs. Barber, had lost her foothold. and was being carried down with her feet off the ground, before the woman fell. {Counsel observes here that Mr Dunne could have quoted the account of the eye-witness Mrs Eliza Jones, but prefers Mrs Barber who was in the melee above and logically could not have seen what happened.]

"Returning to what was occurring at the top of the stairs, there was at the moment when movement forward and into the shelter was arrested, a crowd of about 150-200 outside the shelter and violently anxious to enter it. This crowd was being augmented from minute to minute by fresh arrivals. The immediate effect of the stoppage was to make them press forward harder, and there was an almost instantaneous transition from nervousness and hurry to disorder. There seems to have been an impression among some of the people that they were either being deliberately held back, or that a floodgate situated at the foot of the escalators had been closed against them.

"This continued for some time, probably until about 8.45..., it was not until very shortly after the accident that any police officer arrived. He found the crowd out of hand and went towards the station for assistance. He met three other officers on his way and returned at once with two regular officers, sending an auxiliary back for assistance. These officers did their best to control the crowd and clear the mouth of the shelter, but it was not until the arrival of a sergeant and additional constables that this was accomplished, as near as I can judge, It was about 8.45 p.m. Though panic is not perhaps the proper word to use, there is no doubt that the crowd of from 150 to 200 remaining outside the shelter were out of hand and frantic with nervousness, confusion and worry, which heavier gunfire and further salvos of rockets did nothing to allay...

" At the shelter end of the stair the position was different, but equally tragic. It is the custom at the shelter always to have wardens on duty here to prevent loitering and blocking of the booking hall, and to assist the aged and infirm down the escalators. The flow had been brisk and continuous and all those examined by me agreed that while the people were hurrying and were talking of an expected raid, there was no disorder. There were, or should have been four wardens and a helper disposed in posts between the head of the escalators and the main gate .. The wardens [noticed] an interruption of the flow of persons entering the booking hall [and] cries and screams from the upper stairway.

" All efforts to extricate casualties from the lower side were unavailing until much later in the evening. A police constable off duty came over the heads of the people from the top to the bottom some little time after the accident but was unable to do any good. Some time shortly after 9p.m. a chief inspector, a sub-divisional inspector, and five constables arrived via the emergency exit, but again were unable to extract casualties from the lower end until the pressure had been to some extent eased from above.

"When those capable of moving and most easily moved had been got out from above it was found that the pressure and possibly the pitch of the stairs had produced a strange and terrible result. The bodies of the few still alive and the dead were pressed together into a tangled mass of such complexity that the work of extrication was interminably slow and laborious. This was of course accentuated by the very poor light which could be allowed. The last casualty was not cleared from the stairway until 11.40 p.m.

"Before dealing with the subsequent events of that night I should like to emphasize the speed with which the situation developed. The statements obtained from some 38 witnesses all confirm this: one only gives an account which suggests the contrary. and his evidence I am in any case, for many reasons, inclined to treat with reserve. The stairway was, in my opinion, converted from a corridor to a charnel house in from ten to fifteen seconds.

"I have so far made only incidental references to the police arrangements and dispositions on the night in question... from the outbreak of war and during the winter of 1940-1941, when man power had not become such an acute problem as it is today, the Division was considerably stronger numerically .. it was possible to post men permanently on shelter entrances and at the same time maintain sufficient reserves... [nowadays] the call-up for the services, particularly during the past year or fifteen months, has caused an appreciable reduction in police strength and it became absolutely necessary, in order to maintain mobile reserves available at short notice, to make readjustments of beats patrols, and duties. Permanent posts at shelter entrances have in this division been withdrawn since the summer of 1941, when raiding of the metropolitan area virtually ceased. It is a fact that no incident has hitherto occurred at shelter entrances in this division since the first day of war beyond occasional hooliganism.

"When the alert sounded, constable Henderson, who should have reached this shelter first, was about 660 yards away. He should therefore have been able to get to the shelter entrance within five or six minutes of the alert. In fact he did not do so, and the time at which he estimated his arrival at the shelter both in his statement to his superiors and to me on my first questioning of him, was demonstrably wrong. He did not arrive until after the accident had happened, and that beyond any shadow of doubt was not before 8.27. The same criticism equally applies to the statements of the station sergeant and sergeant MacDonald who took a detail to the shelter, as to the times at which men were sent and the times they left the station. I can find no evidence to suggest that these mistakes in time were anything but bona fide mistakes.

"From 8.30 onwards, I am satisfied that police were despatched to the shelter as rapidly as they became available. Within a few minutes there were a sergeant and ten constables on the spot and this contingent was further and rapidly increased . By 8.45 an Inspector, a sergeant and 15 constables had arrived and thereafter rescue work was organized rapidly and effectively. By about 9.15 there were a chief inspector, two sub-divisional inspectors, an inspector and some sixty constables and sergeants at the scene and further reserves were not concentrated only because they were not required.

32. No one would, I should think, suggest that the results of a fairly searching inquiry into police dispositions and arrangements such as a reference to the transcript of evidence will disclose, is fit matter for general publication. I think, however, I may properly state that as a result of such an inquiry, the opinion I have formed is that the superintendent and his senior subordinates are zealous, experienced and efficient officers, who have organized the policing of the division along lines which experience had hitherto shown would best combine efficiency with the necessary economy in manpower.

"Could the police have prevented this disaster? One must endeavour to forget for the moment the horror and magnitude of the disaster, and to look at the picture as forming part of a much larger canvas. There are in this divisional area some 59 shelters each holding 200 persons or more. Though the tube shelter was by far the most important in the area, every shelter is a potential danger spot.. The police of the division have to make such dispositions as will enable them to meet not one emergency, but very possibly several.

"it is certain that after the reduction in man power which the force has undergone the police cannot be expected to find men on the spot at all points of danger. It is extremely doubtful if this disaster could have been prevented except by the presence on the spot of a number of police anticipating, and numerically adequate to control, a rush by some 450-500 frightened people in the dark. This the police were never in a position to provide.

"Could any steps have been taken by the wardens to avert this accident? The wardens service has been very adversely affected by the "call-up " both in its quality and quantity. I formed the opinion that in their controller, chief executive officer and chief warden, the borough has most competent and conscientious officers but the rank and file appear to have fallen off both in respect of numbers and physique .. Prior to May 29, 1942, the permitted strength of the wardens service was 239: at some time prior to that the numbers had been over 300, and were at that level during the winter 1940-941. On May 29, 1942, the number was reduced to 203, and on June 24 to 160. The present strength is 152, and the service has been unable to keep its strength up to the reduced permitted figure. The post in whose area the tube-shelter is situated is an amalgamation of two former post areas. It covers seventy-two streets and used to have a complement of 100 wardens. The present strength consists of 24 full-time wardens and 29 part-time; including the shelter wardens in the different shelters.

"The tube shelter used to have a staff of a chief shelter warden and deputy and some twelve full-time wardens, besides women wardens. The muster on March 3 in the shelter was the chief and deputy shelter wardens, two wardens on duty in the shelter proper, and four wardens posted for duty between the escalators and the street level. Of these one only was a full-time warden. All these four wardens are advanced in years and of indifferent physique. The disposition of wardens while the shelter was filling and during the alert on March 3 was one man between the main gate and the bottom of the stairs - he was in fact at the bottom of the stairs when the accident happened - two men on duty passing the people from the booking hall down the escalators: and one man on duty near a watertight door close to the office. This man was used by the chief shelter warden or deputy to take messages or give any assistance required there or elsewhere. He was also in the booking hall at the time of the accident. There were no wardens on duty in the street outside the shelter at the time of the accident. The full-time wardens were all at posts or shelters and the part-time wardens were doubtless proceeding to their air raid positions.

36. I am satisfied that no act of commission or omission on the part of any of the staff of wardens was responsible for any part of the disaster, nor in the light of events and in the existing circumstances, could they have done anything to avert it.

"I am satisfied that the chief shelter warden, in so disposing of his wardens, made the most effective use of them in the circumstances. The head of the escalators stands out as the vulnerable point in the interior arrangement of the shelter during the time of ingress. It is a bottle-neck; the capacity of the stairs leading to the booking hall is several times greater than the two escalators leading there from and he was not only justified in so doing, but obliged to concentrate most of his reduced staff there. Had Mr. Edwards, the warden posted to the main gates and stairs, happened by chance to have been at the right place at the right time, I very much doubt if he was physically capable of dealing sufficiently quickly with the woman who fell. Indeed, by the time the press of people immediately in front of this woman had cleared the platform and allowed access to her, it would already, in my opinion, have been too late to do anything.

"The contributory causes of the accident may be separated into two main groups, (i) a psychological change in the attitude of the population towards air raids and shelters generally, and (ii) the physical causes - the borough has some sixty per cent of its public shelter accommodation in this tube, a much larger proportion than any neighbouring borough. This had instilled in the minds of the people a marked preference for this type of shelter, to the exclusion of more easily reached shelters more widely dispersed. Apart from the regular users, a large number of people not in the immediate vicinity of this shelter had come to regard it as a desirable haven to resort to in the event of what might prove to be a heavy raid; [also] a particularly strong apprehension of drastic reprisals for the recent heavy raid on Berlin. This apprehension was fostered by newspaper accounts of the effects of new types of bombs; a realization that new bombing tactics allowed far less time to get under cover and that a raid might be expected to reach its maximum intensity in a very short time. In the new type of raid the air raid warning might precede the bombs by a very short margin; the danger from splinters from our new barrage. The mouth of the shelter stands, as I have said, in a somewhat exposed position; a lack of knowledge of the nature and appearance of the anti-aircraft rockets now in use; The desire of parents to get their children under cover quickly, which induced numbers of people not hitherto users of the shelter to go there before a threatened raid. A very large number of children have fairly lately returned to the area;

All these factors combined to produce

(g) A loss of self control in some hundreds of people attempting to enter the shelter;

(ii) (a) The physical presence of large numbers of children who have come back recently to the area retarded the speed of intake into the shelter, and the speed at which people could reach it;

(b) The shelter has only one entrance. In this it is, if not unique, very exceptional in relation to its size;

(c) The lighting on the stair was very dim, which not only increased the chance of a fall on the stairs, but was bound to cause confusion; however, if a fall occurred, no lighting could, in the circumstances of the present disaster, have prevented that happening which did happen.

(d) There were no handrails down the centre of the stairway. These might have enabled a person falling to save himself. If such a person was burdened with a child in arms and a bundle, as many were, their value would be problematical. If a jam happened despite their provision, they would almost certainly make matters worse. As a contributory cause I attach little importance to their absence;

(e) The absence of a crush barrier, allowing a straight line of pressure from the crowd seeking entrance to the people on the stairs. This was, in my opinion, the main structural defect at the time of the accident;

(f) The main and proximate cause was a sudden rush for the entrance by probably 350-400 people.

"The question as to how far these factors should have been appreciated by the local authority and provided against must be a matter for individual opinion. It is one thing after a fait accompli to make a retrospective analysis such as is contained in this report and that after an exhaustive enquiry into all the matters which have now thrown light on the position. It is quite another to be sufficiently prescient to give the proper values in advance and to take the right action upon them. A fairly simple inductive process enables one to realize now that this accident was more likely to happen at this shelter at this time than previously. Similarly we can say now, that while most of the factors present here are present in other shelters, it is quite certain that not all of them are to be found in any one other shelter and that therefore it was more probable that this accident should happen at this shelter than at any other.

"One must bear in mind that no actual indication of such a disaster had previously been given, and that the physical imperfections of this shelter entrance are exactly reproduced in scores of other tube entrances in the metropolitan area. [Author's note: That statement is flatly contradicted by the testimony of Mr William Joule Kerr, the civil defence technical adviser.] This similarity may well have served to obscure the significance of the exceptional feature here, that this was the only entrance into the largest deep shelter in this part of the metropolis. Further it should be remembered that this was not a specially designed shelter. In the circumstances the local authority had to make the best use of what there was: radical alteration was not a practical possibility.

"[Were] the stairs dangerous, both in nature and their obscurity?. I have come to the conclusion that falls, though perhaps not actually frequent, were not uncommon. The fallen, old women mostly, seemed to regard these petty misfortunes as something to be expected, and to have been quite satisfied to have their hurts attended to at the shelter aid post.

42. I desire now to revert to the question of responsibility, if any, for the disaster on March 3. I should have been content to leave the subject to your consideration very nearly in the shape of my appreciation of the question outlined in paragraph 40, above, were it not for a matter which I must now lay before you.

43. On August 20, 1941, the town clerk, on the instructions of the general emergency committee of the borough, sought authority to incur certain expenditure on work proposed to be done at the entrance of the tube shelter; and to that end, and on that date, sent a letter to the chief administrative officer of London civil defence region enclosing a specification and plan. The relevant item was that the local authority wished to replace, with a brick wall, the wooden paling or hoarding which then surrounded the shelter stairway, which was at that time roofless. After reference to the London passenger transport board, London regional headquarters replied to the local authority on September 27, disallowing a brick surround to the stairway and suggesting that it could be strengthened with salvaged material.

44. The borough replied on September 30, 1941, and included the following passages which I quote verbatim from their letter.

"The general emergency and finance committee at their meeting yesterday gave consideration to your letter of the 27th instant, stating that the regional commissioners were not prepared to approve the scheme for the provision of a surround at the entrance to the Bethnal Green tube shelter.

"The committee were of the opinion that the commissioners could not have been in full possession of the facts in arriving at their decision, and I am desired by the committee to emphasise the circumstances which prompted them to submit their proposal.

"The iron railings of the Bethnal Green gardens link up with two newly constructed brick pillars at each side of the entrance to the shelter, and the structure between consists of a double wooden gate and a small wicket gate at the side.

"The committee are aware, in the light of past experience, that there is a grave possibility that on a sudden renewal of heavy enemy air attack there would be an extremely heavy flow of persons seeking safety in the tube shelter, and that the pressure of such a crowd of people would cause the wooden structure to collapse, and a large number would be precipitated down the staircase.

"As the maximum number of persons which could comfortably be accommodated in the shelter is 5,000, and it is estimated that in a heavy air raid approximately 10,000 people would seek shelter in the tube, it will readily be gathered that a serious problem would evolve in the closing of the shelter to the excess 4,000 unless some strong means of preventing their entry is provided.

"It is not unusual for most of the larger shelters in the borough to empty into the tube shelter during a heavy attack, and the committee feel that there would be the possibility of a serious incident at the entrance to the tube if the responsibility remained with the personnel alone to prevent the overcrowding of the shelter.

"In the light of this further evidence of the need for the erection of a strong gate to the entrance, I am directed by the committee to request that further careful consideration shall be given to the matter, and that approval will be granted to the erection of the gate as suggested.

"I am further directed to add that, in the event of the proposals being again rejected, the committee cannot accept any responsibility for the consequences which might ensue from the lack of adequate protection for the entrance to the shelter."

45. As a result of this letter one of the regional technical advisers inspected the shelter entrance with the then deputy borough surveyor,

and reported as follows: " I have again inspected the approach to this shelter and I am still of the opinion that it would be a waste of money to build up a wall round the steps to prevent the crowd from forcing their way into the shelter, the existing fence with a little stiffening with salvaged timber could be made very much stronger than the gate. If anything is at all likely to be forced it is the gate which I agree might be stiffened with advantage.

"On the other hand the proposal for a covering over the entrance, now put forward for the first time in the town clerk's letter of September 30 is I consider a necessity since, as things are at present during wet weather, rain must pour down the approach steps. I strongly doubt however if anything like three inches of water could possibly ever collect on the landing even after extremely heavy and continuous rain.

"I have discussed this with the deputy borough engineer and he will, I understand, submit a proposal for this cover over the entrance."

46. On October 20, regional hq wrote as follows to the borough:

"With reference to your letter of September 30 regarding the surround at the entrance to the Bethnal Green shelter, I am desired by the regional commissioners to say that they have further considered the matter in the light of a recent report by the regional technical adviser, and they remain of the opinion that it is not necessary to remove the existing fencing and replace it by brick walling.

"The commissioners agree, however, that it is desirable to strengthen the gateway and they also agree to the covering over of the entrance stairway in order to prevent the rain flowing down the stairs into the shelter."

The council's reply, dated October 24 said: " Your letter ... has been considered by the general emergency committee, and I have to inform you that the committee remains of the firm opinion that a brick wall surround at the entrance ... is necessary.

"I am to point out that this facility has been granted in other boroughs in similar circumstances, and to ask that you will be good enough to reconsider your decision in the matter."

47. I think it unnecessary to quote further from the correspondence, copies of which, together with the relevant plans, are attached and marked.

48. It will thus be seen that, as early as August, 1941, the borough appear have contemplated, and to have presented in unambiguous and

clear language, the very disaster which has so startled and shocked them now. It is perfectly true that they regarded as vulnerable a part of the structure whose weakness or strength would have had no effect on the accident as it occurred; but they also realized that pressure was to be expected through the gateway, that is to say, through the very channel by which it was so disastrously exerted on March 3. I attach entirely secondary importance to the remedies which were suggested at this stage for the dangers envisaged. The real significance is that the borough contemplated "a grave possibility of a sudden renewal of heavy enemy air attack"; that there would be. "an extremely heavy flow of persons seeking safety in the tube shelter"; that there would be the possibility of a serious incident at the entrance to the tube if, etc.."

49. It may be suggested that although the letter of September 30 appears to raise the "grave possibility of an accident of the very kind which actually happened, such a possibility was not in fact in the minds of the general emergency committee then having the conduct of shelter affairs. Mr Elsbury, for instance, the chief executive officer of the ARP branch of the borough civil defence, stated that the general emergency committee in making such representations did so "merely from a kind of academic point of view." I should find the greatest difficulty in accepting any such contention. That they intended their observations to be taken seriously is the only inference that I can draw from the passage in their letter in which they disclaim responsibility for "the consequences which might ensue from the lack of adequate protection for the entrance to the shelter". When a body in such a responsible position as a borough is entrusted by statute and moral duty with the task of providing within the resources open to them, adequate protection for their population, they must be taken to mean, and held to abide by, their written word.

50. I think it was unfortunate, as appears from the answers of the (then) deputy borough engineer, that after the question of the specification to be submitted to regional hq had been discussed by the general emergency committee at whose meetings the deputy borough engineer was present, no members of the general emergency committee at any time attended the site with that official to see how he had interpreted their wishes or to discuss with him the problems adumbrated and the solution proposed in his scheme and specification. If the letter of September 30 properly set out the views of the committee,

and it must be taken so to do, it should have been obvious, I think, that the measures proposed were quite inadequate to deal with the danger which was present to the committee's mind.

51. When the regional technical adviser visited the shelter entrance with the deputy borough engineer to consider the latter's proposals, he did so with full knowledge of the contents of the borough's letter of September 30. I am clearly of opinion that that letter, raising as it did certain grave matters concerning an important unit of deep shelter accommodation, should have been treated at regional headquarters as something other than a routine application for the expenditure of public funds. Yet that was, in effect, precisely how it was treated. When the regional technical officer visited the site he omitted to consider any of the graver implications of the borough's letter or to turn his attention to the question how far the borough engineer's proposals were adequate to deal with the dangers suggested. He is perfectly frank in admitting that he would regard it as part of his duties to condemn or criticize proposals which did not seem to meet any particular problem raised. I should find it hard to accept any other interpretation of his duty ... Whether the responsibility for tendering such advice lay on him alone or whether there is any other official at regional hq whose duty it is to satisfy himself that once such an issue is raised it receives proper attention, I have not considered it necessary to inquire. That seems to me to be purely a matter for regional headquarters and ultimately for the minister, if my view is correct. I regard the omission as unfortunate.

52. It seems to me to be unnecessary, and beyond the terms of my reference, to attempt to assess at any length the comparative responsibilities of local authorities and regional commissioners. That upon the former rests a primary responsibility imposed both by statute, moral duty and common sense is, I think beyond dispute. They and they alone, by their opportunity for intimate knowledge of their own problems, must be the body responsible for their solution, if that is possible. But it is, I think, quite clear from the nature of the delegation of the minister's powers to regional commissioners, that in clothing them with authority to give directions, there is imposed a duty to give such directions when such directions are necessary, and if and when as in the present case a particular matter is brought to their attention, which from its nature is such that the power to give directions may have to be exercised there is a duty (quite outside and collateral to the

primary duty cast on the local authority) to see that proper advice is tendered when the need for it is shown; and also that if such advice is disregarded, a direction logically follows. Should there be any confusion on this point, there is a danger that the public will fall between two stools. I think the position was set out quite clearly in home security circular No 133/1940 of June 15, 1940, but a lot of paper has rolled over the presses since then, and it may be that a reminder, and if necessary, a clarification of the position would not now be out of place.

53. I wish it to be clearly understood that I limit my criticism of the conduct of the general emergency committee and of regional headquarters to this: that each, a matter of great importance having been raised, failed to see that it was properly understood and considered by their technical officers. It by no means follows that the steps which might have been taken in the light of the experience gained up to that date would have been those now suggested or that they would have been adequate to prevent the accident which has occurred.

54. During the course of my enquiry a certain volume of criticism was directed to the internal administration of the shelter and in one instance at least, charges of corruption, entirely unsupported by any evidence, were made against the local authority. As to the latter, if they are ever formulated in such a way that a reply is possible, no doubt they will receive attention. As to the former, they can only be brought within the terms of reference to me in so far as they relate to matters which may have contributed to the accident on March 3. One only, I think, merits mention in any detail.

55. It appears that during the air raid alert on January 17 the watertight door situated at the foot of the escalators, and giving access to the shelter proper, was closed, or partially closed, while a number of persons were coming down the escalators. The result, though not attended with casualties, did produce a potentially dangerous situation at the time, and there is evidence to show that on March 3 some people at the shelter entrance and on the stairs thought that the same thing had happened again. I would recommend that the procedure regulating the opening and closing of this door should be carefully examined and that the most precise orders should be issued on the subject.

56. While it would be unfair to suggest, from the statements made involving criticism of the administration of this shelter, that the administration was unsatisfactory, evidence that it was noticeably

efficient is equally nebulous. The bulk of such criticism came from sources which, however honest in intention, were plainly coloured by political motives and personal animus. and came mainly from persons who for one reason or another had ceased to be employees of the borough authority; but at the same time certain matters, such as the wearing of uniform by wardens on duty, the checking of periods of duty, the recording of messages, and the precise definition and allocation of duties, may have tended to be regarded as automatic rather than requiring constant supervision. I trust, therefore that I may go outside the strict terms of reference to recommend that the borough authority and the regional commissioners should, without delay, assure themselves that nothing is neglected to secure the highest efficiency in this extremely large and important shelter.

While I am touching upon these points, may I go one step further? This accident in this particular borough has tended to become an acute point of political controversy. This is most unfortunate and may well lead to an attempt in certain quarters to weaken the position of the borough as the responsible authority. The chief and deputy shelter wardens are both members of the council. The allocation of executive positions and offices of profit to elected members of local authorities has been regularised by section 10 of the local government staffs (war service) act of 1939, but none the less I feel that, save in exceptional circumstances, there are strong arguments against such a practice, and it is right, I think, to draw attention to the question.

57. In so far as the circumstances of this accident are an index of circumstances to be considered for the future, the steps and modifications taken and made, should afford as effective a safeguard as practical possibilities permit. The entrance to the shelter has been altered to include a covered way leading to the stairs. This will permit of adequate lighting of the stairs and of the approach to them. The stairs have been divided into three lanes by two sets of handrails, and direct pressure into the covered way is controlled and prevented by a crush barrier.

58. The most outstanding internal weakness of the entrance system is also receiving attention. A third escalator is to be fitted with treads or otherwise adapted to carry passengers. This will diminish the potential bottle neck in the booking hall, and should bring the carrying capacity of this part of the system into line with the capacity of the

intake, modified as it will be by the crush barrier.

59. I have already stated that the police have reinstituted a permanent post at the entrance to the shelter which will be continued until a further decision is taken.

60. I put forward a suggestion to the chief engineer of the ministry of home security, the chief executive officer, the chief warden, and the superintendent of police, among others, which I think may merit consideration. It is that, in those shelters whose nature or length of approach make it of vital necessity, in case of need, to arrest the movement of those in motion in or to the shelter, there should be installed a signal controlled by wardens or those in charge of the shelter, the object of which is to convey to those seeing it that they must stand fast until further instructions. A series of red lights visible at all points between street and shelter level is the sort of thing I have in mind. Their effectiveness would, of course, depend upon how far their purpose was known to those in a position to see them, and would involve some education of the shelter users. 61. It would appear prudent, in view of the possibility of a similar situation arising at any large deep shelter to consider the following points:

(a) The possibility of protecting, the entrance from direct pressure by a crush barrier. Such a barrier should be sufficiently high to be obvious to persons well back in a crowd. A low barrier cannot be seen and is a grave danger as the crowd may continue to push not realizing the obstruction. It goes without saying that the barrier must be substantial; the pressure which a crowd may exert is enormous. If a rush by a crowd is a possibility, the barrier should be erected at such a point that police can at least deal with the trouble on level ground. No gate can be shut against a press of people; bostwick or sliding gates may be useful if space is limited but a solid and obvious barrier wall is almost certainly the most satisfactory.

(b) Entrances should where possible be so screened that stairways and the like can be properly lighted.

(c) The provision of handrails should at least be considered. In a lighted way they should be a help.

62. May I conclude with two short propositions?

(a) This disaster was caused by a number of people losing their self control at a particularly unfortunate place and time.

(b) No forethought in the matter of structural design or practicable police supervision can be any real safeguard against the effects of a loss of self control by a crowd. The surest protection must always be that self control and practical common sense, the display of which has hitherto prevented the people of this country being the victims of countless similar disasters.

I should like to thank the mayor and town clerk. of the borough for their kindness and for the excellent arrangements made for the holding of this inquiry. I should like also to thank Superintendent Hill for the most efficient way in which he arranged for the attendance of large numbers of witnesses at extremely short notice, and greatly expedited the hearing. Mr. I. Macdonald Ross, who acted as secretary conducted all the arrangements most admirably, and I am deeply indebted to him not only for them but also for valuable suggestions as to, and information for the purposes of, this report.

```
I am, Sir,
Your obedient Servant,
L. R. DUNNE. March 23, 1943.
```

# APPENDIX C

Here is the list of persons who gave evidence at the official inquiry, conducted by Mr Laurence Dunne, at Bethnal Green town hall (present: Mr Dunne, Mr I Macdonald Ross (secretary)) .

First day - Thursday, 11th March

Superintendent Hill
Mr Charles Edwards
Alderman Key
Chief Inspector Harris
S D Inspector Jannaway
Mr. Edward Ernest Jolly
Mr Percival James Bridger
S D Inspector Hunt
Inspector Ferguson

Second day - Friday, March 12

Mr J Lowe
Mr S A Bryant
Mr R Cotter
P. Sgt F Swindells
P.Sgt R MacDonald
P.Const J Henderson
P. Const J. Stubbington
Sir Wyndham Deedes
Mr S Elsbury
Mr A W Hastings

Mr E Schleich
P.Sgt. Sonfield
P.Const. King

Third day - Saturday, 13 March

Dr Summers
Mrs I A Peel
Mr M P Wilson
Mr J C Edwards
Mrs M. Barber
Mr W Steadman
Mrs M E Reeve
Miss J K Bennett
Mrs I Brent
P. Const. Holton
P.Const.Davenport
Mr J Knowles
Mrs R Lewis
Mrs M Crabbe

Fourth day - Monday, March 15

Mrs A Bryant
Miss E Bryant
Mrs C Bryant
Dr M. Long
Dr E White
Mr C H Cunningham
Mr S R Bagshaw
Mr F H W Leveridge
Mrs M S Johnson
Inspector Hunt (recalled)
Dr M E Weber
Mr J N Nardone
P.Const. Hooper
L/Bdr W L Meikle
P.Const. T Penn
Dr J B Cook
Dr R I Clipstein
Dr Mary Elizabeth Wehner
Dr Alfred Prentice
Mrs M G Roe
Mrs H Dabbs
Mrs E Reynolds
Mrs W MHill
Mrs E Jones
Mrs L Hilditch
Mrs C Brown.

Mrs M Lock.

Fifth day - Tuesday, March 16

Mr W Strother, borough engineer
Sir A M Rouse (ch. engineer, home security)
Mr W J Kerr (reg. technical adviser)
Mr W C Johns
Mr G Johnson
Mr J W Gaites
Mr I Myers
Mr W Lawson
Mrs E. Lawson
Dr Morgan Kavanagh
Mrs R A Gerrard
Miss V Stocks
Mrs J Weddell
Mr B Ramsey
Mr J E Quorn
Pte. J Crawley
P. Const. Henderson (recalled)

Sixth day - Wednesday, March 17

Mr J E King
Mr H Papworth
Mrs L Ward
Mr J Bridger
Mr A W Hastings

Eighty-four people gave evidence, four were called back for further clarifications.

.